A SPORTI

W H

MOOSE AND TROUT

A B O U N D

To:
Ralph
Best Wishes
Mike Parker

NIMBUS
PUBLISHING

MIKE PARKER

Nimbus Publishing Limited
P.O. Box 9301, Station A
Halifax, Nova Scotia B3K 5N5
(902) 455-4286

Design: Kathy Kaulbach, Halifax
"Blessing on the Woods" by Arthur Guiterman, N.S. Dept. of Natural Resources
Cover marbled paper: Thomas West, Paros Marble Co.
Printed and bound in Canada

Canadian Cataloguing in Publication Data
Parker, Mike.
Where moose and trout abound
Includes bibliographical references.
ISBN 1-55109-132-1
1. Hunting–Nova Scotia. 2. Fishing–Nova Scotia. 3. Tracking and trailing–
Nova Scotia. I. Title.
SK152.N6P37 1995799.29716C95-950220-3

Note to the readers: In recognition of contemporary sensibilities, the publisher takes responsibility for the change or deletion of several words that appeared in the original documents. The presence of both British and American spelling is explained by the different affiliation of the authors. The excerpts collected here have been copy edited for consistency and clarity, with the aim of preserving as much as possible the original spellings and punctuation. Some idiosyncrasies remain.

CONTENTS

THE HERITAGE OF THE CHILDREN

Dad, your gun is in its case,
Your rod hangs on the wall;
Daddy, when you shooted ducks,
Did you shoot 'em all?
When you killed the deer and fox
And cut the balsam tree,
Couldn't you have saved a few
Fer Billy and fer me?

Dad, your factory's on the creek
And makes a lot of noise
Churning up the water,
Where we swimmed when you were boys.
Daddy, when you built it there,
Couldn't you maybe
Just have saved a swimmin' hole
Fer Billy and fer me?

Daddy, wouldn't you suppose
That if you really tried
You could save a little woods
And field and countryside?
Kinda keep a savin' up,
You and Uncle Lee,
Just a little out of doors,
Fer Billy and fer me.

Joe Rogers
Secretary, Nova Scotia Guides' Association
1955

PREFACE

*The wild scenery of the forest, the magic beauty of the lake, the health which accom-
panies the sportsman in spite of exposure or frequent saturations, the knowledge that
the moose is reposing unconscious of your presence and murderous intentions at no
great distance and that the glassy lake or wild, rocky river teems with the finny tribe—
all contribute to render a camp life in Nova Scotia as agreeable and exciting as the
lover of wild life and wild scenery can desire.*
Campbell Hardy, 1855

These are the images that can be easily kindled as one reflects before
the crackling campfire on the shores of some backwoods lake or
scans the accounts of early sportsmen, all the while longing for a
return to those utopian times. Much has changed in Nova Scotia
since Campbell Hardy's day. Moose no longer "repose" in significant
numbers, our lakes and rivers have ceased to "teem" with trout and
salmon, and the "wild scenery of the forest" has been all too often
replaced with "dreary clear cut, or by spindly third- and fourth-
growth scrub woodland." Yet, in retrospect, it is evident that there is
much truth in the proverb that the more things change, the more
they stay the same.

Campbell Hardy's writings, and those of fellow British officers
garrisoned at Halifax in the nineteenth century, are filled with tales of
bountiful game and pristine wilderness. However a somber tone
underscores the enthusiasm of these earliest sportsmen. All was not
well in the woods and waters. Moose and caribou were slaughtered
for marketable hides and meat; forest fires ravaged fragile habitat;
poor milling practices and poachers wreaked havoc on streams and
rivers. Such was their concern that Canada's first game protection
society was formed in Nova Scotia in the 1850s, and laws were legis-
lated to curb the wanton destruction.

Although this society was sound in principle, it lacked clout and a
scientific base in managing renewable resources; caribou were
doomed to extinction by the early 1900s and nearly sixty years have
passed since the last provincial moose hunt. However, for all the
apparent doom and gloom, Nova Scotia was widely famed as a sporting mecca into the post-World War Two years, when the reintro-
duced white-tailed deer of the 1890s had, by then, bridged the gap

left by their antlered cousins; a daily bag limit for the "finny tribe" was still virtually guaranteed; and the devastation of industry had not yet scarred the hinterland.

The fathers of conservation, like Campbell Hardy, and their early successors may be excused for shortcomings on the grounds of well-intentioned ignorance. No such allowances can be made in recent years. All too often those entrusted as caretakers have succumbed to the inherent human frailty of greed. The result has been obvious. Now, more than two hundred years after the first laws were enacted in Nova Scotia to protect lands and forests, a renaissance is under way that will hopefully forestall those who reap profits while raping the land. Amid talk of biodiversity, natural landscapes and ecosystems, corridors, stewardship and lost heritage, "the Department of Natural Resources has undertaken a systematic assessment of the natural areas of Nova Scotia in order to identify new areas for protection. Thirty-one areas, totalling some 287,000 hectares, have been proposed as candidate protected areas. Nova Scotia's commitment to establish a parks and protected areas plan responds to direction provided at global and national levels, and parallels similar initiatives undertaken by other Canadian provinces and territories. These commitments to set up protected area systems consistently stress a 'call to action.' They convey a sense of urgency in protecting selected natural areas that remain intact before the option to do so is lost forever." ("A Proposed Systems Plan for Parks & Protected Areas in Nova Scotia," Newsletter; Nova Scotia Department of Natural Resources, 1994.)

Is there reason for optimism? The skeptics hope that actions will speak louder than words. Nova Scotia currently ranks eighth out of the twelve Canadian provinces and territories in the percentage of protected crown land. The new plan will see protected areas rise from 2.9 per cent to approximately 8 per cent of the provincial total. Since approximately one-half of Nova Scotia's forested land is owned by the private sector, and not the Crown, one must also hope that lands and forests outside these designated spaces will not be ignored in terms of resource management. Only time will tell.

Where Moose & Trout Abound is a companion book to my first, *Guides of the North Woods,* in which the rise and demise of guiding in Nova Scotia is documented primarily through oral history gathered from the last of the old-time woodsmen. It tells of "the growth of the tourist industry in Nova Scotia [which] has been closely identified down through the years with many old timers, whose colorful personalities and skill with the rod and gun drew thousands of regular visitors from far and wide. These men who helped the industry in its infancy were of the true pioneer stock. They opened the land ... discovered the lakes and streams where the speckled trout were plentiful, and knew of the endless lucrative game trails. This virgin paradise was theirs, not to exploit but to make use of and develop. And this they did. Those were the days when men moved into a wilderness, and hacked out their claim from the solid timberland." (*The Chronicle-Herald,* (Halifax), February 13, 1950.)

Continuing that story, *Where Moose & Trout Abound* parallels the guiding accounts but from the perspective of the sports' recollections. Portrayed in photos and prose gathered mainly from private and archival sources, this book focuses on what must be considered the halcyon days of hunting and fishing, from Campbell Hardy's era to the late 1930s—a period, regardless of foreboding, that had so much to offer when compared with today's remnants. Perhaps Farish Owen, age ninety-four, summed up the changes best when he lamented upon reflection during a 1986 interview for the guides book, "That's just fairy tale now."

Many of the trips chronicled here were through or on the periphery of parts of Nova Scotia that have already been or are designated to become protected areas and parks, such as Kejimkujik, Rossignol, Tobeatic, Tangier-Liscomb, Margaree-Middle rivers, and the Cape Breton Highlands. The authors, British and American sports, tell of the beauty of the land, the sport, and the men who led them, while they laugh at their own foibles. No excuses are made for romanticizing the past; it is part of our history, our heritage. Gone should not mean forgotten. Sportsman Arthur P. Silver echoed today's sentiments in 1907 when he wrote, "We are all more or less susceptible to a sort of nostalgia for the woods and wilds, where life may be lived in perfect accordance with nature's demands."

CHAPTER 1

MONARCH OF THE FOREST

How cold it is! The fire must be out again! "Joe!" I shouted, from under my blanket. "Hi, Paul!" But it was of no use. Indians are not easily awoke at night and can sleep through any amount of cold; so, seeing that the exertion of making up the fire myself would be less than that of awakening the Indians, I flung off my covering, and sat up. It was yet night, and the stars still peeped brilliantly through the massive branches of the firs overhead. Of the enormous fire we had made previously to our falling asleep, nothing now remained but a few live embers, gleaming from under the charred black log.

Drawing on my moccasins, I stepped over the prostrate figure of my companion, and, after a few minutes groping round the camp, returned with a supply of dead wood and birch-bark.

Veteran Micmac bear hunter Christopher Paul (1825-1905), wife Margaret Babaire (d. 1902), and possible grand-daughter, ca. 1900. Paul lived most of his life at Shubenacadie, N. S., and would surely have been a guide for the British officers of Halifax.

Presently, a cheerful blaze once more illumined the little encampment, and the stems of the surrounding pines. Certainly the camp was a very primitive one. A few sweeping fir branches veiled our heads from the wind and dew, and some of the more delicate fibre, spread on the ground, served as our couch. The two Indian hunters, their heads pillowed on their coats, slept undisturbedly on the opposite side of the fire, and at my feet lay the blanket-covered figure of my companion of the rifle.

Crouching over the renewed blaze, I lighted the continually used comforter of the sojourner in the woods—the old clay pipe—and entered upon a train of reflection. The night frosts of October have again tinted the deciduous foliage of the Nova Scotian forest with scarlet, yellow, and orange and all the denizens of the woods and streams, with one exception, may well rejoice at this glorious season. That exception is the monarch of the forest—the stately moose. Yes, the fall has arrived, and the sport of hunting the moose may be legitimately resumed. The forest, at this season of the year, rendered marvellously beautiful by the brush of the painter, Autumn, and not yet deserted by the migratory birds, offers most interest to the lover of nature. The bull moose, too, is in his pride; his head is adorned with massive antlers, now at their full growth; he is perpetually on the move, and if perchance he hears the distant lowings of his consort, or the crafty imitation produced by the Indian hunter through his trumpet of birch-bark, the usually silent forest echoes with his hoarse, short bellowings. Give me the fall for moose-hunting, the stealthy creep in the wild country, in the hazy atmosphere of an Indian summer day, or the "calling" on the moonlit barren.

Each puff of the fragrant smoke recalled to my memory some passed incident, till, like the cloud which I had created, and which floated quietly around me in the calm air, all the details of our excursion as yet experienced became connected, and evident to my awakening senses.

The spot, which we had made our resting place for the night, was in the neighbourhood of the beautiful Missigomis, the Fish Lake of the Ship Harbour country. After a tedious ride of nearly fifty miles, we had taken to the woods. The whole of the previous day had been occupied in trudging under heavy loads over a difficult barren country, covered with the remains of the ancient forest, now prostrate from the effects of fires, and through deep swamps and across streams overgrown with tangled brakes of underwood and briars. Right glad were we when, at length, we changed our rough walking, so painful to the moccasined foot, for the luxury afforded by treading on the soft elastic moss, which everywhere carpeted the ground under the noble fir forests, and when the sight of the first fresh impression of the monarch of the woods informed us that we had gained the hunting country, extending nearly fifty miles to the eastward, uninterrupted by a settlement.

Besides, I longed to witness the autumnal glories of Missigomis. I love to revisit old scenes, particularly when associated with the enjoyment of good sport and success, with either the rod or the rifle. Two years previously I had spent a glorious ten days in the woods around the Fish Lake. Though both the forest and the lake were bound up in the icy chains of a Nova Scotian midwinter, I had perceived that the scenery of Missigomis in the fall of the year must be beautiful. I felt that these woods were old acquaintances. Perhaps I had trudged through the deep snow, in our long daily excursions from camp, under those very fir boughs, which now wave overhead in the eddies caused by the ascending heat.

Then, as I sit and smoke, and gradually grow warm and comfort-

able and drowsy again over the night fire, I love to listen to the nocturnal sounds of the forest, the melancholy and deep-toned hoot of the great horned owl, or the strange, demoniac laughter of the barred owl, the distant scream of the wary loup-cervier, or a sudden distant crash in the forest, which makes your heart leap as you know it is the moose on his nightly wanderings, and makes you long for morning to be on the trail.

But the pipe is soon out, and sleep comes again to my aid; so, falling back on the boughs, and drawing the blanket over me, I contribute in a short time, as I have no doubt, to our small private chorus of forest music.

"Captin, Captin, day comin'. I tink we try call this mornin'."

It was old Joe Paul, our head Indian, who stood over me, and endeavoured to rouse me with his foot and voice.

"Come, most ready, Captin? The other gentleman won't go—too lazy."

"All right, Paul, I'm ready"; and jumping hastily to my feet, I gave myself a hearty matutinal shake. I disengaged the rifle from the blanket, which it had shared with me during the night, and after a draught of cold tea remaining in the kettle from our last meal, followed the old hunter into the indistinct gloom of the forest.

"But, Paul," said I, as we felt our way through the dense bush, "I'm afraid the moose are scared away from this neighbourhood by the smell of our fire, and the noise caused by chopping the fire-wood last evening."

"No, I guess not; pretty calm last night—the smoke go up quite straight. May be no moose round here yesterday; this mornin', perhaps, plenty moose, quite handy. Bull moose travel great deal at night this time of year."

Emerging from the dense forest, we stood on a small barren, covered with laurels and mosses, all crisp and white with hoar-frost.

"Guess we make the call here; grand mornin' this for call. You sit down," said Paul, in a subdued voice, and pointing to a prostrate stem, which lay, half hidden, amongst the rank laurels.

The mellow and rarely enjoyed light of a clear calm morning, preparatory to sunrise, had now overspread the whole sky, and unveiled the beauties of the landscape—the scene of our operations. The barren was a natural one, not one of those dreary and rugged

tracts of country strewn with bleached granite boulders, and distort-
ed black trunks, which cover you with soot as you brush against
them, and testify of the merciless fires, which have, from time to
time, vied with the destructive, though less wanton axe of the white
man, in his encroachment on the primeval forests of America; but a
little arena, surrounded by the dense fir foliage, as a wall, and carpet-
ted with high tufts of white moss and ground laurel. The white moss
is constantly found in large patches on upland, barrens, and in the

open country, and is the almost sole food of the caribou. It grows in
tufts of more than a foot in height and dome-shaped, and its intricate
ramifications are very beautiful—resembling those of coral.

Our barren was at a considerable elevation above the surrounding
country, and, gently sloping between two lofty ridges, covered with
hard-wood. Through a broad opening at its lower end, a magnificent
view of a wild undulating forest country burst upon us. Impenetrable
gorges, choked up with a dark growth of hemlock and pine, separated the serpentine ridges, which were covered with rolling masses of
maples and birches.

The beams of the now rising sun, here and there, among the long shadows of the hills, lit up the beautiful autumnal hues, greatly deep-ened by the frost of the preceding night, of the deciduous foliage. Here and there, too, stationary sheets of mist, as yet in shadow and undispelled by the sun-beams, veiled the forest lakes.

Many miles distant, and beyond the chaos of foliage, a dull uni-form grey tint proclaimed the immense wilderness of burnt barrens over which we had trudged painfully for a whole day; and in the extreme horizon, and tinted with hazy blue, rose up the Musquedoboit hills, indistinct, light coloured patches on their sides shewing the clearings of the settlement. Here, save the snap of a twig as the old Indian cautiously ascends a tree, no sounds disturb the peace of the primeval forest, other than the voices of nature from time immemorial.

The edges of the barren are now alive with birds chirping joyous-ly, and hopping out from the obscurer recesses of the foliage to the extremities of the sunlit branches. A host of the noisy and inquisitive chickadee birds, so called from their note, swarm around me almost venturing on my shoulder in their anxiety to determine my genus. An owl noiselessly flits into the top branches of a pine, and descends hop by hop into its obscurer shades, perhaps the author of the star-tling hootings I had listened to in the night. There is a little chirp at my side, and looking round, I see, prancing about at the end of the trunk on which I sit, a squirrel, evidently in a high state of excite-ment and wrath, his tail erect and bristling like that of an enraged cat. A movement of my arm and he is off like an arrow, glancing through the frosted laurel of the barren. Presently a wrathful rattling chirrup attests his presence in a distant spruce.

But now my attention is called to old Paul who has settled himself in the top branches of a tall fir. Applying the birchen trumpet to his mouth, he commences the three prolonged and plaintive notes—the cry of the cow moose: "Quoo-o-o-o-h—quoo-o-o-o-r-h—quoo-o-o-rr."

Away flies the startling sound, echoing through the forests. What sacrilege to disturb the peace of those beautiful morning woods by a sound so loud, and so strangely wild! All is quiet again, and we hold our breath in our eager listening.

Suddenly Paul and I look at each other. We had both heard it. I hear it again, and this time quite plain.

"Quoh, quoh, quofh."

It is an answer. Paul at once drops his call into the laurels, and rapidly descends the tree.

"How far is he off, Paul? How far is he off?" whispered I, fumbling in my excitement for a fresh cap.

"Quite handy, not more than quarter mile away. Come here, and no move till I tell you," said the Indian, dragging me quickly back to a clump of young spruces behind, in which we crouched for shelter from the quick sight of the wary brute.

For nearly ten minutes we moved not a limb. At length, Paul stood up and made another call. Again the moose answered, but his responses were suddenly ended by a sound that emanated from a hard-wood hill before us, as if a stick were rapidly and fiercely drawn over a line of rails.

"What on earth can that be Paul?"

Disappointment was plainly expressed in the Indian's countenance, as he replied, "Oh yes, the brute. Oh very bad job this. You hear um rattle um horns?"

"Yes, Paul; another moose, I suppose."

"Sartin. No good to call any more. Moose no come up now, they 'fraid of one another; they 'fraid of the fight."

It was as old Paul supposed, not another sound could either moose be induced to utter, and the thoughts of a good breakfast partly smothering my disappointment, I followed the Indian back to camp.

After a hearty breakfast on pilot-bread and fried pork, eaten on broad sheets of that useful material, birch-bark, with a sharpened stick in one hand, and the belt knife in the other, we fixed the loads, and shouldering them, "made tracks" for the Missigomis.

A walk through the forest, under heavy loads, is generally a tedious and silent affair. At long intervals, the Indians exchange a few syllables in their melodious language and impressive manner. Their subdued tones draw no echo from the woods, as does your quick and boisterous exclamation. Though they have no intention of hunting, should they find tracks quite fresh, their step is as light, and their caution as unrelaxed as on the trail. In fact, either when hunting, or merely travelling through the woods, they avoid disturbing, in any way, game that might be in the neighbourhood of their route.

A three hours' walk through evergreen woods of a fine growth and we discerned the sparkling water through the trees in front, and presently, to our great relief, threw off the loads on the banks of a picturesque stream.

It was a lovely spot. Where we came upon it, the brook dashed over and between dark masses of rock, and expanded into a small basin, in which were reflected the bright autumnal hues of the overhanging bushes. An old canoe, turned over, lay on the opposite bank, a welcome sight to us, for on the finding of this canoe depended, in a great measure, our chance of success on the Missigomis.

An old canoe, turned over, lay on the opposite bank.... She was in a very bad state–the alternate frosts and suns of two years had opened the seams, and the bark hung in rags from the ribs.

Presently, the Indians, bounding over the stream from rock to rock, had commenced a strict examination of her condition. She was in a very bad state–the alternate frosts and suns of two years had opened the seams, and the bark hung in rags from the ribs.

"Guess we try make job of it," said Paul, as they started back into the forest with drawn knives. Indians are seldom overcome by any obstacle in the practice of wood-craft; and in a few minutes–during which we had set up a light rod, and were flinging bright trout out of the water to our heart's content–they returned, with a supply of spruce gum.

They simmered it over a small fire in one of our tin plates, and plastered it with the moistened hand over the yawning seams. The larger rents were covered by pieces of rag soaked in the composition. In half an hour she was in the water, old Paul standing up in her in triumph.

"Grand," said he. "Guess we take whole moose in. Now we go to lake right away."

The stream was deep, and nothing was to be feared from sub-merged rocks. The vigorous strokes of the broad paddle impelled the canoe in rapid strides past the steep wooded banks, and, suddenly rounding a point, we found ourselves in full view of the magnificent expanses of Missigomis. The Indians withdraw their paddles, and placing them across the canoe, lean on them to survey and enjoy the well remembered scenery.

The panorama is too extensive, and the colouring too gorgeous to be comprehended by the eye at once. What contrasts there are in the tints of the massive foliage—the most vivid scarlet bordering on ver-nal green, the intense blue of the lake setting off the glories of the orange-coloured masses, which here and there sink into it, and the carmine of the cranberry bushes which everywhere fringe its shores. And how beautifully the bright tints are toned down towards the extremer distances, by the hazy warmth of the atmosphere. Innumerable islands, glowing like gems, dot the surface of the lake, and masses of bare rock, in some of which, resemblances to uncouth animals may be traced, rise starkly from the water. What a contrast to the scene as I remembered it in midwinter. Where we now glide over the calm, dark water, I had then walked securely on firm ice, the drifting snow hissing past my feet, and those richly coloured forests were then only dimly visible, and in leaden-coloured outline through the darkened atmosphere.

Notwithstanding the gumming to which she had been subjected, our canoe leaked badly, and as we paddled lustily across the lake towards a distant bay, the Indians constantly looked at the increasing depth of water in her, and shaped their course so as never to be very far from islands or rocks.

At length we reach our destination—a little cove shaded by over-hanging maples, and where water-lilies and various aquatic plants, undisturbed by storms, grew luxuriantly. As the bow of the canoe buries itself in the cranberry bushes on the shore, we jump out and I, impatient to revisit the scene of my old encampment, leave the party to unload the canoe, and rush forward into the forest.

I soon find the old path. Ah, here is an old moose foot, and I presently come upon a moose skin, stretched between two stems. Under a gigantic hemlock, which from its size had braved the axe of the camp woodcutter, stands the old bark tenement. Brave old camp!

Not a sheet of bark has moved. Many a joyous evening has been spent under those sheltering poles, many a moose steak cooked over blazing logs, and many a hunting story and incident of the day's sport recounted merrily, while reposing on those once soft fir boughs, which, dead and brown and shrivelled now, strew the ground inside.

But here come the Indians, and active preparations must end my reflections.

Several days passed, and though we traversed the neighbouring forests during the day, and, aided by the canoe, visited the remoter parts of the lake, and

'Camp Frost,' Sixth Lake, Digby County, ca. 1890s. L-R: Bear River Micmac guides Johnnie McEwan, ?, John Labrador and two unidentified sports. Johnnie McEwan wrote the following for a 1926 guide booklet Fishing & Hunting in Nova Scotia: *"When the rod and rifle are not in use there are other pastimes for the sportsman to do such as taking pictures of wild game. Running rapids, with canoes, bathing, and if you have an Indian Guide with you he will learn you to be an expert shot with bow and arrow. Hair-raising bear and moose stories by the camp fires. I was very successful last season (1925) in hunting and fishing. I am enclosing photos which will speak for themselves written on back of pictures."*

called in the evenings, as yet no moose meat had been brought to camp.

Fortune had not favoured us in creeping, and many a moose had been started without a shot. The Indians informed us that it was a bad fall for calling. The moose, though readily answering the call, would not come up. Either they were too numerous, and feared each other, or they suspected all was not right.

One morning, I was about to discharge my rifle, which had remained loaded for several days, and sent our younger Indian to make a fresh blaze with his axe, in the trunk of a hemlock about a hundred yards from the camp, as a mark. He was about to lift his

How the pulse is stirred on a bright October morning as the prow of the yellow canoe cuts the gently resisting current, rifles all aboard, together with a few days' frugal rations.
Arthur Silver, 1907

axe, when, bounding suddenly aside, he ran quickly back, pointing towards a dense under-growth of spruce, on the right of the old tree.

I saw, from the waving of the boughs, that something was moving quickly through the shrubbery towards us. What could it be? Nothing, surely, but a moose. We were all present, and knew that no other encampment was in the neighbourhood. It must be a moose; and I had levelled the rifle, intending to fire, the instant the creature should shew itself clear of the copse.

Most fortunately, my finger was stayed. The branches parted, and forth strode the figure of a young Indian, his blanket strapped on his back, and carrying his gun and powder-horn. I instantly recognized in him an old friend. He was old Paul's son, and had hunted for us, in our winter sojourn in these forests. He had followed our tracks from the settlements to the head of the lake, and, guessing where he should find us, walked round the shore to the old camp—a distance of not less than ten miles, owing to the intricate ramifications of the lake.

As soon as he had regaled himself with a hearty meal, he became communicative.

"Oh, my sakes!" said he. "The moose shocking plenty up round the Stillwater. See plenty fresh tracks—some only gone by this mornin."

"Well, Jim, are you a good hand at calling?"

"Guess pretty grand—call good many moose one time and another," replied Jim.

"Very well. As soon as you have rested, you shall go with me to the Stillwater, for the evening's calling. I am glad you have come. May be, you will bring us good luck; and we want to taste fresh meat very badly."

About three hours before sundown, we all left the camp, my companion, with old Paul, going down the lake in the canoe whilst the two young Indians accompanied me through the woods to the Stillwater. The Stillwater proved to be a stagnant, muddy stream, flowing into the lake through swampy fir woods. The dark valley through which it passed was overlooked, on either side, by lofty hard-wood hills. The ground, in this thickly-shaded valley, was carpeted by wet moss, the numerous impressions on which showed that it was a favourite resort for the moose.

When we arrived, it was our intention to await sundown, and then ascend the hills to call, but we could not resist the inviting appearance of the tracks in the moss, and, as there was nearly an hour's daylight, we commenced to creep. The rank moss greatly favoured our stealthy manoeuvring, and for some time we wound along through the valley, examining recent tracks and the cropped underwood. Presently, Joe, stooping down and examining a track with unusual earnestness, beckoned to his comrade. They had a short conversation, in tones almost inaudible, accompanied by gesticulations evidently illustrative of the manner in which the moose were working. As I joined them, Jim whispered: "Quite fresh track, two bull and cow, they gone by just ten minutes. See here," said he, bending down a young maple shoot bitten off at about ten feet from the ground. "See where he make the fresh bite."

It was cropped evidently quite recently, for on breaking it off an inch lower down, no difference in colour could be perceived between the fracture, and where the moose had bitten it.

"I tink you put on cap, no tellin' when we see um moose now."

Now begins the creeping in earnest. Jim takes the lead; we follow in Indian file. Caution is needed, at every step, and in the greatest degree. Here is a tanglement of branches in our path. Every twig must be carefully handled, that it may not snap or fly suddenly back. A long undulation in the rank moss shows the position of the fallen tree beneath. We carefully avoid stepping on it. It might be rotten, and give way with a fatal crash. Especially have we to care, as we worm our way through the thickets, that our guns may not clash against the dense stems. All the faculties of the Indians are on the alert. Their eyes are searching the thickets in every direction. Mine have enough employment in looking where to plant my foot, and what to avoid.

At intervals we find large cavities where the swamp has been torn up, and masses of moss and black mud scattered around, by the bull moose. Suddenly a distant sound strikes our ears, and we stand listening in our tracks. It is repeated—a wild roar—and appears to come from over the hill on our left.

"The moose!" said Jim, and clearing the swamp we dash up the hill side, the energetic waving of Jim's hand, as we arrive at the summit, warning us to exercise our utmost caution. Yes, we are right! The brutes are in the valley beneath, and the forest echoes with the deep guttural bellowings of the antlered monster, and the plaintive answers of his consort. There is a crash! A dead tree has been laid prostrate. The clattering din of his horns, as they come in contact with the timber, show the progress of the bull.

I never felt such excitement on the trail. I have crept on moose, and shot them while standing in unsuspecting repose, or while dashing in alarm through the woods; but to follow behind such an uproar of bellowings, the crashing of falling timber, and rattling of antlers, was grander than anything I had before experienced. Yet we in no way relaxed our former caution. We could not depend for any mistake on our being concealed by the tremendous uproar of the moose, and our course must still be shaped with due observance of the wind.

We descend the hill obliquely to the edge of the Stillwater, across which the moose have just swum. The mud stirred up by them in their passage is still eddying in the stagnant water. With careful steps, on the certainty and firmness of each of which depends not only our coming upon the moose undisturbed, but also the chance of a tremendous ducking, we cross the water on a dead trunk, fallen from bank to bank.

We gain on our quarry. My nostrils become sensible of an over-powering odour of musk, which clings to every bush they have brushed past; and endeavouring to penetrate the thickets ahead for a sight of the game, we advance rapidly. Suddenly and unexpectedly we leave the dense underwood, and stand on the edge of a little open valley. Jim, as I emerge from the thickets immediately after him, bounds on one side, his arm extending and pointing.

"Fire," he hissed. "Fire quick."

I see there is an enormous black mass standing behind a group of young maples at the further end of the little valley. The antlers! It is the bull! Something crashes away into the woods on my right, but I heed it not; my gaze is rivetted on that gigantic dusky form which is slowly beginning to move. In a second the sight of the rifle bears upon him, and the surrounding forest reverberates with the unwonted report. Uttering an appalling roar, the huge brute sinks, plunging into the laurels.

With a shout we rush on. To our astonishment he rises, with another fearful roar, and before I have time to check my speed and level the rifle once more, he has disappeared in the thickets.

"Come on," shouts Jim, "we sure to get him—he badly hit."

There is no tracking now; the crashing branches, and the roars of the enraged animal direct us, and we dash through swamps, and bound over fallen trees with desperate energy. But it is of no use; the pace was too good to last, and presently, torn and exhausted, we flung ourselves at full length on the moss, and for a while listen to our own deep breathings, and to the hoarse bellowings of the rapidly retreating moose momentarily growing fainter.

Joe, the youngest Indian, a lad of extraordinary endurance, has taken my rifle, and renewed the chase by himself.

Perhaps nowhere are there better moose-callers to be found than the Micmac Indians of Nova Scotia, the older men far excelling the younger. There is something peculiar to the Indian speech, abounding as it does in soft vowel sounds, which lends itself readily to the imitation of every sound of nature.

Arthur Silver, 1907

"Most rested?" asked Jim, after a long pause. "Guess we try a call." "What, call after the fearful disturbance we have been making in these woods? What can you be thinking of, eh Jim?"

"Oh, the moose never scare for the firin' this time of year; we go on little piece and try," said the Indian, picking up his musket, and leading the way.

Presently we came out of the bush, and stood on the edge of an enormous barren. The woods at the extreme end were barely visible, from the distance and the decreasing twilight. Two horned owls flew from a dead tree in front, uttering the most appalling yells. Jim scrambled up into the top branches of a spruce fir to commence immediate operations.

He called, and to my taste made a most admirable imitation of the cry of the cow moose. The echoes had just died away, and all was quiet again, excepting the screechings of the disturbed owls, and the still audible bellow of the wounded moose, when we heard the distant report of a gun emanating from a hilly, hard-wood country on our right.

"Jim," said I, aloud, "Joe has shot him. Come down—I am sure we cannot get an answer now. It is getting quite dark, and Joe will never find us."

Jim, however, made no answer, but impatiently waved for me to be silent, appearing to be listening intently. In a second or two, he rapidly descended the tree, and softly stepping up to me, whispered:

"Put on cap—two moose comin—one there, other there," pointing first towards the country we had just left, and then to the dim outline of forest across the barren. "One pretty handy," said he, "not more than tree hundred yards, may be."

I would scarcely have believed it possible, from my previous knowledge of the caution, and extraordinary and sometimes unaccountable penetration of moose at other seasons of the year; but in a few minutes I certainly distinctly heard the quiet grunt of a bull moose, at a comparatively very short distance.

In about ten minutes, Jim gave another call, which drew more decided and louder answers from the bull. We heard the twigs snap, and the rustling of his feet in the laurels. He seemed to be making a *detour*. Suddenly he uttered a roar, the counter-part of the sound uttered by the moose I had wounded, and crashing through the thicket, left us no hope of obtaining a shot at him.

"Bad job, Jim," said I.

"Oh, sartin. I 'most afraid when I hear um first, he would fix us. He come across our tracks, and started when he smell um—very angry, very mush disgust. Here come Joe," replied the Indian, pointing towards the middle of the barren.

Looking in the direction, I saw in the indistinct light of the young moon, which was now smiling behind the trees, a dark figure approaching us, his lower part completely obscured by the rank mist exuding from the swampy ground. Presently he was with us, and cast himself down, as if exhausted, on the wet moss. There was no sudden questioning of "have you shot him?" or, "how did you find us?" I took up his gun, and found a piece of meat bound on to the barrel. That was enough, and Jim at once commenced calling again. At first, there was no answer. The country was quiet again, and our straining ears could detect nothing, except the occasional chirrup of a snake in a swamp, and that curious rushing sound of music—an indescribable melodious rustling in the calm atmosphere, with which the ear of the moose-caller becomes so well acquainted, yet so unconscious of its cause.

Though it was very cold, and my damped limbs were stiffened under me from crouching so long in the same posture, I could not but enjoy the calmness and beauty of the night. The moon was now down very low, but the columns of a magnificent aurora, shooting up to the zenith, threw a mellow light on the barren, which, covered by mist as by a sheet, appeared like a moonlit lake, and the numerous little clusters of dwarfish spruce as islands. We had not heard a moose answer to our call for nearly an hour, and were preparing to move, when the distant sound of a falling tree struck our ears. It

It is difficult to exaggerate the startling appearance of the gigantic North American moose— the largest and most powerful of the deer tribe now extant— when the spectator for the first time encounters him in his native haunts.... When he is in the act of charging, or in one of those fits of fury which frequently take possession of him, his aspect may be described as almost terrific.

Arthur Silver, 1907

appeared to come from the dim outline of forest, which skirted the barren on our left, and at a great distance.

Down we all drop again in our deeply impressed couches to listen. The sounds indicate that moose are travelling through the woods, and close on the edge of the barren. Presently, the foremost moose is abreast of our position, and gives vent to a wild and discordant cry, more approaching to a yell than any other sound. This is the signal for a general uproar amongst the procession of moose, for a whole troop of them are following, at long and cautious intervals.

The timber is crashing loudly opposite to our position, and distant reports show that more are still coming on in the same direction. A chorus of bellowings responds to the plaintive wail of the cow. The branches are broken more fiercely, and horns are rapidly drawn across stems as if to whet them for the combat. Momentarily I expect to hear the crashing of rival antlers. One by one, the bulls pass our position, and I long to get up and dash into the dark line of forest, and with a chance shot scatter the procession; but to do so would entail wanton disturbance of the country, so we patiently wait till the last moose has passed.

Never before had I heard the calmness of the night in the Nova Scotian forest so disturbed. They had passed as a storm, and now the barren and the surrounding country were once more enveloped in the calm repose of an autumnal night. The night's calling was now ended, and we might talk unreservedly.

"Now, Joe," asked I, "tell me how you shot the moose."

"Well," said he, "when I leave you, I run very hard for 'bout a mile—moose make great noise—I know he very sick, and soon, when I come on little barren, I seen um standin on other side. Oh, my sakes! He got such a bad cough! He not able to hold up his head. Then I shoot, and he run a little piece further, and drop. You want to know where you hit um? Well, I tell you. You hit um in the neck—make um cough shocking."

It was now perfectly dark, and, as we had nothing to eat, and had no blankets with us, I could not help wishing to be snugly extended on the boughs in the well-warmed camp, distant some five miles, in a straight line through the woods.

"Jim," said I, "can we manage to find our way back to camp to-night?"

"I got notion, myself, 'bout that," said Jim. "I just thinking we try. Very dark though. We make plenty torch, when we come to birch wood."

For about a mile, we felt our way in almost total darkness, through very thick greenwood. Obstacles and difficulties seemed to be ten times as numerous as in the day. The stems were often so thick that we could not force our bodies between them, and we were greatly embarrassed by windfalls. I heard a squirrel chirp in a tree, and did not take any notice of it. The Indians, however, stopped, and had a very serious dialogue together.

"What's the matter, Jim?" I asked.

"You hear um squirrel? Well, in all my life, I never before hear squirrel cry at night; no more did Joe. The old people all say, it is very bad sign. We don't like to hear the squirrel at night."

Indians are very superstitious, and regard unwonted sights and sounds in the woods with great awe and dislike.

To our great relief, we at length came to a hard-wood country; and peeling broad sheets of bark from the birches, rolled them up into torches. One of these was at once lighted, and, by its cheerful, blazing light, we again proceeded, with much more ease and sureness of foot.

The torch held aloft by the foremost Indian, illuminating the colossal stems of the white birches, produced a grand effect. The light, though it shewed us where to tread, placed all beyond its circumscribed glare in mysterious blackness, and it appeared wonderful on the part of the Indian, that he could shape his course with such unerring judgment.

As we approached the camp, the Indian's call, in resemblance of the cat-owl, was answered by his father, and in a few more moments, we were relating to

There are indescribable charms in the life of a hunter in the woods. Apart altogether from the fact of sport and its consequent excitement, there is a singular pleasure and sense of freedom in this life, which require to be felt and enjoyed, before they be understood. There are so many appeals to the fancy, to the taste—ay!—even solemn ones to the soul, which even the dullest mind cannot resist. There are certain irksome cares and ties in civilization, which do not control one in the woods. Francis Duncan, 1864

attentive, and, perhaps, slightly envious ears, the incidents of the day's chase.

Early next morning we started with all our appointments in the canoe, paddling up an arm of the lake not far from the extremity of which lay the dead moose. We were provided with the salt requisite for preserving the whole carcass. Leaving my companion and old Paul at a little distance from the water, to make a primitive camp, I followed the two young Indians to the spot where lay the dead moose.

I must say I had feelings of awe and compunction, as I came near the spot where the noble creature had fallen. Carrion moose-birds, always at hand on such an occasion, screaming horribly, and flitting from tree to tree, guided us to the moose. I experienced quite a shock, when I at length momentarily caught a glimpse of his black hide between the thick fir boughs, and I rushed forward with impatience. He lay on the moss of a sloping hill, in an attitude of wildly picturesque collapse, and a broad dark-stained line on the moss shewed his course from the spot where the fatal bullet had struck him. Myriads of blue-bottle flies swarmed around the carcass, and whilst the Indians performed the butchering process, I lighted several fires around, to keep off these noisy and troublesome visitors.

It was a noble moose—black as jet—and exceeded my expectations, as regarded size, and the development of the antlers. When the head was severed from the body, I could not raise it from the ground.

What savoury odours arose from the frying-pan, which cooked that morning's breakfast! How many times was it loaded, again and again, with massive steaks! It was our first taste of fresh meat since we had left the settlements, and the venison—without the least savour of the musk which the animal, when alive had exuded so power-fully—was tender and delicious. At length the feast was over, and the broad plates of birch-bark, on which we had eaten, blazed fiercely in the fire.

"Feel pretty smart, now," said old Paul, as he wiped his broad hunting-knife on the sleeve of his blanket-coat. "Most able to carry quarter of moose out to settlement. All ready? Well, we go all hands and fix the meat."

We all took part in the work, and the beautiful little barren was temporarily deformed by becoming a forest shamble. First, the hide was suspended in the form of a bag, which was fastened by numerous withe tyings to cross-poles between the stems of three white birches. Into this, the meat, cut into blocks and well-sprinkled with salt, was firmly packed, and lastly the whole was thatched over with boughs to keep the meat from the birds, and the effects of the sun.

Bringing with us the head, divested of all superfluous flesh, the shanks, and as much meat as we could carry, we returned to camp to spend the rest of the day in repose, having determined to start for the settlements next morning. The marrow-bones, which had been baked in the ashes all night, and the brisket, which had been suspended over the wood smoke, were luxuries for our last breakfast in the woods.

And well did we need a good breakfast, for a weary walk was before us, and under great loads. The least, which one of us carried, could not have been less than forty pounds. Placing everything in the old canoe, we paddled five miles down the lake. As we drew her up and turned her over in the cranberry bushes, we could not help entertaining feelings of gratitude at the opportune services rendered by the old craft. Poor old canoe! Though she was half full of water when we stepped out, old Paul promised to bring a good supply of rosin when he should return for the meat—"fix her up grand a'most," said he.

Where we had disembarked was the extreme end of the lake; and a few steps into the dense bush placed an impenetrable barrier of evergreen branches between our eyes and its picturesque and smiling expanses. I always, in leaving the woods, entertain a melancholy satisfaction in saying farewell and casting lingering glances back at old scenes—the camp, with the well-known stems of the adjacent woods. How often have I looked back at the light fabric, and thought how

Unidentified sportsman and Indian guide, ca. 1922.

sad it would be to find it prostrated by the fierce winter storm, and at the still ascending column of blue smoke from the dying fire, and wondered how long it would last after the farewell shout of its retiring kindlers had died away, and how shortly the moose, or the lucifee would stride over its charred logs!

We kept on gallantly for ten miles through the forest, Jim and the other young Indian carrying the massive head by turns. At last, we arrive at the shore of Big Ship Harbour Lake, and, procuring a settler's boat, sailed down it some fifteen miles before a refreshing breeze, and arrived at sundown at the road which skirted its lower extremity. I pitied the poor Indians as we walked eight miles on the execrable road with our loads. They are never very good at walking on the bare rocky road, though they so infinitely excel in travelling through the wild country.

The next day, two waggons bore ourselves, Indians, and the magnificent head triumphantly into Halifax, where our stories and our steaks were discussed with infinite relish by numerous admirers.

IRVIN S. COBB

American
sportsman, 1926

HUNTING MISE

At the outset, when our expedition was still in the preparatory stages, we collectively knew a few sketchy details regarding the general architectural plan and outward aspect of the moose. One of us had once upon a time, years and years before, shot at or into—this point being debatable—a moose up in Maine. Another claimed that in his youth he had seriously annoyed a moose with buckshot somewhere in Quebec. The rest of us had met the moose only in zoos with iron bars between us and him or in dining-halls, where his head, projecting in a stuffed and mounted condition from the wall, gave one the feeling of dining with somebody out of the Old Testament. Speaking with regard to his family history, we understood he was closely allied to the European elk—the Unabridged told us that—and we gathered that viewed at a distance, he rather suggested a large black mule with a pronounced Roman nose and a rustic hat-rack sprouted from between his ears. Also, through our reading upon the subject, we knew that next to the buffalo he was the largest vegetarian in North America and, next to man who believes in the forecast of a campaign manager on the eve of an election, the stupidest native animal that we have. By hearsay we had been made aware that he possessed a magnificent sense of smell and a perfectly wonderful sense of hearing, but was woefully shy on the faculty of thought, the result being that while by the aid of his nose and his ear he might all day elude you, if then perchance you did succeed in getting within gunning range of him, he was prone to remain right where he was, peering blandly at you and accommodatingly shifting his position so as to bring his shape broadside on, thereby offering a better target until you, mastering the tremors of eagerness, succeeded in implanting a leaden slug in one of his vital areas.

But, offhand, we couldn't decide what the plural of him was. Still if the plural of goose were geese and the plural of mouse were mice, it seemed reasonable to assume that the plural of moose should be mise. Besides, we figured that when we returned and met friends and told them about our trip it would sound more impressive, in fact more plural, to say that we had slain mise rather than we had slaughtered moose. In the common acceptance of the term as now used, moose might mean one moose or a herd of them, but mise would

Author Irvin Cobb, left, with Runyon at Red Lake camp, Annapolis County, ca. 1926.

mean at least a bag of two of these mighty creatures and from two on up to any imaginable number.

One mentally framed the conversation:

"Well, I hear you've been up in Canada moose-hunting." This is the other fellow speaking. "Kill any moose?"

"Kill any moose? Huh, we did better than that—we killed mise."

So by agreement we arranged that mise it should be. This being settled we went ahead with our plans for outfitting ourselves against our foray into the game country. We equipped ourselves with high-powered rifles, with patent bedding-rolls, with fanciful conceits in high boots and blanket overcoats. We bought everything that the clerk in the shop, who probably had never ventured north of the Bronx in all the days of his sheltered life, thought we should buy, including wicked looking sheath knives and hand axes to be carried

Sportsmen Colonel Tillinghast Houston and Harry Leon Wilson, Red Lake.

in the belt, tomahawk fashion, and pocket compasses. Personally, I have never been able to figure out the exact value of a compass to a man adrift in a strange country. What is the use of knowing where north is if you don't know where you are? Nevertheless, I was prevailed upon to purchase a compass, along with upward of a great gross of other articles large and small which the clerk believed would be needful to one starting upon such an expedition as we contemplated. On my account he did a deal of thinking.

By past experience I should have known better than to permit myself to be swept off my feet by this tradesman's flood of suggestions and recommendations. Already I had an ample supply of khaki shirts that were endeared to me by associations of duck-hunting forays in North Carolina, and chill evenings in an Adirondack camp, and a memorable journey to Wyoming, where the sage-hen abides. I treasured a pair of comfortable hunting-boots that had gone twice with me to European battlefields, and down into the Grand Canyon and up again and across the California desert, without ever breeding a blister or chafing a shin. Among my most valued possessions I counted an ancient shooting-coat, wearing which I had missed quail in Kentucky, snipe on Long Island, grouse in Connecticut, doves in Georgia, and woodcock in New York State. Finally, had I but taken time for sober second consideration, I should have recalled that the guides I have from time to time known, considered themselves properly accoutred for the chase when they put on the oldest suit of store clothes they owned and stuck an extra pair of wool socks in their pockets. But to the city-bred sportsman, half the joy of going on a camping trip consists in getting ready for it.

That clerk had a seductive way about him; he had a positive gift. Otherwise I suppose he would have been handling some line which practically sells itself, such as oil stocks or mining shares. Under the influence of his blandishments I invested in a sweater of a pattern which he assured me was being almost exclusively favored by the really prominent moose-hunters in the current season, and a pair of corduroy hunting-pants, which, when walked in, gave off a pleasant swishing sound like a soft-shoe dancer starting a sand jig. I was particularly drawn to these latter garments as being the most vocal pants I had ever seen. As I said before, I bought ever and ever so many other things; I am merely mentioning some of the main items.

We assembled the most impassive group of guides in the whole Dominion—men who, filled with the spirit of the majestic wilds, had never been known publicly to laugh at the expense of a tenderfooted stranger. They did not laugh at Harry Leon Wilson's conception of the proper equipment for a man starting upon such an excursion as this one. Wilson, on being wired an invitation to go on a hunt for moose, promptly telegraphed back to the best of his recollection he had not lost any moose, but that if any of his friends had been so unfortunate or so careless as to mislay one, he gladly would join in the quest for the missing. He brought along an electric flashlight, in case the search should be prolonged after nightfall, a trout rod and a camera. The guides did not laugh at Colonel Tillinghast Houston's unique notion of buying an expensive rifle and a hundred rounds of ammunition and then spending his days in camp sitting in his tent reading a history of the Maritime Provinces in two large volumes. They did not laugh at Colonel Bozeman Bulger's overseas puttees, or at Damon Runyon's bowie knife, or at Major McGeehan's eight-pound cartridge-belt—it weighed more than that when loaded, I am speaking of it, *net*—or at Frank Stevens' sleeping-cap or at Bill Macbeth's going-away hair-cut—the handiwork of a barber in a remote village, who plainly was a person looking with abhorrence upon the thought of leaving any hair upon the human neck when it is so easy to shave all exposed surfaces smooth and clean from a point drawn across the back of the head at the level of the tops of the ears on down, as far as the rear collar button. He must have been a lover of the nude in necks, that barber. The guides did not laugh even at my vociferous corduroys, which, at every step I took, went *"Hist, hist,"* as though entreating their wearer to be quiet so they might the better be heard.

By a series of relay journeys we moved up across the line into Quebec, thence back again below the boundary and across the State of Maine, thence out of Maine into New Brunswick and to the thriving city of St. John, with its justly celebrated reversible falls which, by reason of the eccentricities of the tide, tumble upstream part of the time and downstream part of the time, thence by steamer across that temperamental body of water known as the Bay of Fundy, and so on into the interior of Nova Scotia.

If anywhere on this continent there is a lovelier spot than the

Vast, indeed, is the number of lakes scattered broadcast over Nova Scotia—often connected by streams into long chains—

affording means for delightful expeditions, by means of a birch-bark canoe or light draught boat, far into the penetralia of the backwoods.

Arthur Silver, 1907

southern part of Nova Scotia in midfall I earnestly desire that, come next October, someone take me by the hand and lead me to it and let me rave. It used to be the land of Evangeline and the Acadians; now it is the land of the apple. You ran out of the finnan-haddie belt in and around Digby into the wonderful valley of the apples. On every hand are apples—on this side of the right-of-way, orchards stretching down to the blue waters of one of the most beautiful rivers in America (the Annapolis), on that side, orchards climbing up the flanks of the rolling hills to where the combing of thick timber comes down and meets them; and everywhere, at roadside, on the verges of thickets, in pastures and old fields, are seedlings growing singly, in pairs and in clumps. They told us that the valley, scenically considered, is at its best in the spring after the bloom bursts out upon the trees and the whole country-side turns to one vast pink and white bridal bouquet, but hardly can one picture it revealing itself as a more delectable vision than when the first frosts have fallen and every bough of every tree is studded with red and green and yellow globes and the scent of the ripened fruit rises like an incense of spices and wine.

The transition from the pastoral to the wilderness is abrupt. You leave Annapolis Royal in a motor car—that is, you do if you follow in our footsteps—and almost immediately you strike into the big game country. Not that the big game does not lap over into the settlements and even into the larger towns on occasion, for it does. It is recorded that on a certain day a full-grown moose—and a full-grown moose is almost the largest full-grown thing you ever saw—strolled through one of the principal streets of St. John and sought to enter—this being in the old sinful times—a leading saloon. But such things as these do not happen every day. To meet the moose where frequently he is and not merely where occasionally he is, one must go beyond the outlying orchards and on into the vast expanse of the real moose country—hundreds of hundreds of miles of virgin waste, trackless except for game trails and portages across the ridges between waterways. It is a country of tamaracks and hemlocks, of maples and beech and birch, of berries and flowering shrubs, of bogs and barrens and swampy swales, of great granite boulders left behind by the glaciers when the world was young and thawing, of countless lakes and brawling, white rapids and deep blue pools where, in the spawning season, the speckled trout are so thick that the small trout have to travel on the backs of the larger ones to avoid being crushed in the jam. I did not see this last myself; but I saw all the rest of it—the woods wearing the flaunting war-paint colors of the wonderful Canadian Indian summer—crimson of huckleberry, tawny of tamarack, yellow of birch, scarlet of maple; the ruffed grouse strutting,

Nova Scotia is admirably adapted to the moose, because her lakes are studded with little thickly wooded islets where the cow moose hides away her fawns, and because the long chains of swamps and mossy bogs, which run far back into the heart of the evergreen woods, abound with their favourite browse, and while secluded, at the same time these open spaces are free from the encumbrance of dense timber.

Arthur Silver, 1907

unafraid as barnyard fowl and, thanks be to a three-year period of protection, almost as numerous as sparrows in a city street; the signs of hoofed and padded creatures crossing and criss-crossing wherever the earth was soft enough to register the foot tracks of wild things.

And if you want to know how New Brunswick looked after Nova Scotia, you are respectfully requested to reread the foregoing paragraph, merely leaving out some of the lakes and most of the boulders.

On a flawless morning in a motor boat we crossed a certain lake, and I wish I knew the language that might serve to describe the glory of the colors that ringed that lake around and were reflected, to the last flame-tipped leaf and the last smooth white column of birchen trunk in its still waters, but I don't. I'll go further and say I can't believe Noah Webster had the words to form the picture, and he had more words than anybody. As for myself, I can only say that these colors fairly crackled. There were hues and combinations of hues,

The first leg of the journey completed in the comfort of a motor boat, the work of portaging now begins.

shadings and contrasts such as no artist ever has painted and no artist ever will care to paint, either, for fear of being called a nature faker.

The scene shifts to our main camp. We have met our guides and have marveled at their ability to trot over steep up-and-down hill portages carrying, each one of them, upon his back a load which no humane man would load on a mule, and have marveled still more when these men, having deposited their mountainous burdens at the farther end of the carry, go hurrying back across the ridge presently to reappear bearing upon their shoulders upturned canoes, their heads hidden inside the inverted interiors and yet by some magic gift peculiar to their craft, managing somehow to dodge the over-hanging boughs of trees and, without losing speed or changing gait, skip along from one slick round-topped boulder top to another. Now we are in the deep woods, fifty miles from a railroad and thirty miles from a farmhouse. We sleep at night in canvas lean-tos, with log-fires at our feet; we wash our faces and hands in the lake and make high resolves—which we never carry out—to take dips in that same frosty water; we breakfast at sun-up and sup at dusk in a log shanty set behind the cluster of tents, and between breakfast and supper we seek, under guidance, for fresh meat and dining-room trophies.

We have come too late for the calling season, it seems. In the calling season Mr. Moose desires female society, and by all accounts desires it mightily. So the guide takes a mean advantage of his social cravings. Generally afoot, but sometimes in a canoe, he escorts the gunner to a likely feeding-ground or a drinking place and through a scroll of birch-bark rolled up in a megaphone shape, he delivers a creditable imitation of the call of the flirtatious cow moose. There are guides who can sound the love note through their cupped hands, but most of the fraternity favor the birchen cornucopia. The sound—part lonely bleat, part plaintive bellow—travels across the silent reaches for an incredible distance. Once when the wind was right there is record of a moose-call having been heard six miles away from where it was uttered, but in this case the instrumentalist was a Micmac Indian, the champion moose-caller of Nova Scotia and perhaps of the world.

In the bog where he is lying, or on the edge of the barren where he is feeding, the bull hears the pleading entreaty and thereby is grossly deceived. Forgetting the caution which guides his course at other times, he hurries where the deceiver awaits him, in his haste smashing down saplings, clattering his great horns against the tree boles, splashing through the water-brooks. And then when he bursts forth into the open, snorting and puffing and grunting, the hunter beholds before him a target, which in that setting and with that background looms like a grain elevator. Yet at a distance of twenty yards or thirty, he has been known to miss the mark clean and to keep on missing it, the while the vast creature stands there, its dull brain filled with wonder that the expected cow should not be where he had had every vocal assurance she would be, and seemingly only mildly disturbed by the crashing voice of the repeater and by the unseen, mysterious things which pass whistling over his back or under his belly as the gun quivers in the uncertain grasp of the over-anxious, buck-ague-stricken sportsman. Once, though, he has made up his sluggish wits that all is not well for him in that immediate vicinity, he vanishes into deep cover as silently as smoke and as suddenly as a wink.

The mating time comes in mid-September and lasts about a month more or less; and since the open season does not begin until October the first, it behooves the hunter who wishes to bag his moose with the least amount of physical exertion on his own part to be in camp during the first two weeks of October, for after that the

bull moose is reverting to bachelorhood again. He may answer the call, but the chances are that he will not. A little later on, after the snows have come, one may trail him with comparative ease. Besides, he is browsing more liberally then and consequently is moving pretty constantly. But between the time when the leaves begin to fall and the time when the snow begins to fly, he is much given to staying in the densest coverts he can find and doing the bulk of his grazing by night.

So he must be still-hunted, as the saying goes, and it is still-hunting that we are called upon to do. The guide takes his birch-bark horn along each morning when he starts out, carrying it under one arm and an ax under the other, and upon his back a pouch containing the ingredients for the midday lunch and the inevitable fire-blackened teapot, which he calls always by the affectionate name of "kittle." He never speaks of stopping for lunch. When the sun stands overhead and your foreshortened shadow has snuggled up close beneath your feet like a friendly black puppy, he suggests the advisability of "biling a kittle," by which he means building a fire and making tea. So the pack between his shoulders is largely ornamental; it is habit for him to tote it and tote it he does, but mainly he depends upon his eyes and his ears and his uncanny knowledge of the ways of the thing we aim to destroy.

Yes, they call it still-hunting and still-hunting it truly is so far as Louis Harlowe or Sam Glode, the Micmacs, or Charley Charlton, the head guide, is concerned, as he goes worming his way through the undergrowth in his soft-soled moccasins, instinctively avoiding the rotted twig, the loose bit of stone and the swishy bough. But the pair of us, following in his footsteps, in our hard-bottomed, hob-nailed boots, our creaky leather gear and our noisy, waterproofed nether garments, cannot, by the widest latitude in descriptive termi-nology, be called still-hunters. Carrying small avalanches with us, we slide down rocky slopes which the guide on ahead of us negotiated in pussy-footed style; and we blunder into undergrowth; and we trip over logs; and we flounder into bogs and out of them again with loud, churning sounds. Going into second on a hillside, we pant like switch engines. I was two weeks behind with my panting when I came out of Canada and in odd times now I still pant briskly, trying to catch up.

Milford House guide Charlie Charleton kneeling with rifle and moose call to right of unidentified sport. Charlie was not only head guide for Cobb's hunting trip but also the immortal guide Charles the Strong in Albert Bigelow Paine's book The Tent Dwellers.

Reaching level ground we reverse gears and halt to blow. Toward midafternoon, on the homebound hike, our weary legs creak audibly at the joints and our tired feet blunder and fumble among the dried leaves. We create all the racket that, without recourse to bass drums or slide trombones, it is humanly possible for a brace of overdressed, city-softened sojourners to create in deep woods, and still our guide—that person so utterly lacking in a sense of humor—speaks of our endeavor as still-hunting. If an ethical Nova Scotian guide—and all professional guides everywhere, so far as I have observed, are most ethical—were hired to chaperon Sousa's band on a still-hunt through the wilderness and on the way Mr. Sousa should think up a new march full of oom-pahs and everything, and the band should practice it while cruising from bog to barren, the guide, returning to the settlements after the outing, would undoubtedly refer to it as a still-hunt.

In our own case, I trust that our eagerness in some measure compensated for our awkwardness. At least, we worked hard—worked until muscles that we never knew before we had, achingly forced themselves upon our attention. Yet, if for the first day or two our exertions brought us no reward in the shape of antlered frontlets or great black pelts drying on the rocks at the canoe landing or eke savory moose steaks in the frying pan; if it seemed that after all we would have to content ourselves with taking home a stuffed guide's head or so; if twilight found us reuniting at the supper table each with tales of endless miles of tramping to our credit but no game, nevertheless and notwithstanding, the labor we spent was not without its plenteous compensations.

To begin with, there was ever the hope that beyond the next thicket or across the next swale old Mr. Sixty-Inch Spread would be browsing about waiting for us to come stealing upon him with all the stealthy approach of a runaway moving-van and blow him over. There was the joy of watching our guide trailing, he reading the woods as a scholar reads a book and seeing there plain as print what we would never have seen—the impress of a great splayed hoof in the yellowed moss, the freshly-gnawed twigs of the moose-wood, the scarred bark high up on a maple to show that here a bull had whetted his horns, the scuffed earth where a bear had been digging for grubs, the wallow a buck deer had made at a crossing. And when he told us that the moose had passed this way, trotting, less than an hour before, but that the deer's bed was at least two nights old, while the bear's scratching dated back for days, we knew that he knew. Real efficiency in any line carries its own credentials and needs no bolstering affidavits. There may be better eyes in some human head than the pair Louis Harlowe owns or than that equally keen pair belonging to Harry Allen, the dean of New Brunswick guides, but I have yet to see their owners, and I am quite sure that for wood-craft there are no better equipped men anywhere than the two I have named.

We couldn't decide which was the finer—the supper at night with a great log fire chasing back the dense shadows and the baked beans and the talk and the crisp bacon and the innocent lies passing back and forth, or the midday lunch out in the tangy, painted forest, miles and miles away from anywhere at all, with the chickadees and the snow-birds and the robins flittering about, waiting their chance to gather the crumbs they knew we would leave behind for them and with the moose-birds informally dropping in on us before ever the kettle had begun to sing.

Naturalists know the moose-bird, I believe, as the Canada jay and over the line in the States they call him the venison hawk, but by any name he is a handsome, saucy chap, as smart as Satan and as impudent as they make 'em. The first thin wisp of your fire, rising above the undergrowth, is his signal. For some of the denizens of the wilderness it may be just twelve o'clock, but to him it's feeding time. Here he comes in his swooping flight, a graceful, slate-blue figure with his snowy bib and tucker, like a trencherman prepared. And there, following close behind him, are other members of his tribe. There always is one in the flock more daring than the rest. If you sit quietly, this fellow will flit closer and closer, his head cocked on one side, uttering half-doubtful, half-confident cheeps until he is snatching up provender right under your feet or even out of your hand. His preference is for meat—raw meat for choice, but his taste is catholic; he'll eat anything. Small morsels he swallows on the spot; larger tidbits he takes in his bill and flies away with to hide in a near-by tree crotch. His friends watch, and by the time he has returned for another helping they have stolen his cache, so that chiefly what he

Frank Stevens wearing his hunting/sleeping (?) cap, Red Lake camp.

gets out of the burden of his thriftful industry is the exercise. I do not know whether this should teach us that it is better to strive to lay by something against a rainy day and take a chance on the honesty of the neighbors or to seize our pleasure when and where we find it and forget the morrow. Aesop might be able to figure it out, but, being no Aesop, I must continue to register uncertainty.

Campfire suppers and high noon barbecues and glorious sunrises and shooting the rapids in the rivers and paddling across the blue lakes, scaring up the black duck and the loons from before us, and all the rest of it, was fine enough in its way, but it was not killing the bull moose. So we hunted and we hunted. We dragged our reluctant feet through moose bogs—beaver meadows these are in the Adirondacks—and we ranged the high ground and the low. Cow moose we encountered frequently and calves aplenty. But the adult male was what we sought.

We had several close calls, or perhaps I should say he did. One of our outfit—nameless here because I have no desire to heap shame upon an otherwise well-meaning and always dependable companion—had been cruising through thick timber all day without seeing anything to fire at. Emerging into an open glade on a ridge above Little Red Lake, he was moved to try his new and virgin automatic at a target. So he loosed off at one of the

Colonel Bozeman Bulger bedecked in his overseas puttees; Bill Macbeth stands to the right in background.

big black crows of the North that was perched, like a disconsolate undertaker, with bunched shoulders and drooping head, on a dead tamarack fifty yards away. He did not hit Brother Corbie but he tore the top out of the tamarack snag. And then when he and his guide had rounded the shoulder of the little hill and descended to a swamp below they read in certain telltale signs a story which came near to moving the marksman to tears.

Moving up the slope from the other side the guide had been calling, a bull moose, and a whaling big one, to judge by his hoof marks, had been stirred to inquire into the circumstances. He had quitted the swamp and had ambled up the hill to within a hundred yards of the crest when—as the guide deduced it—the sound of the shot just above caused him to halt and swing about and depart from that neighbor-

A successful 'mise' hunting trip. James W. Stuber hunting party, Milford House, ca. 1913. Stuber was the assistant chief for the Ohio Bureau of Fish and Game. Famed Micmac guide Louis Harlow stands third from left.

hood at his very best gait. But for that unlucky rifle report he probably would have walked right into the enemy. My friend does not now feel toward crows as he formerly felt. He thinks they should be abolished.

An experience of mine was likewise fraught with the germs of a tragic disappointment. In a densely thicketed district, my guide, with a view to getting sight of the surrounding terrain above the tops of the saplings, scaled the steep side of a boulder that was as big as an ice-house and then beckoned to me to follow. But as a scaler I am not a conspicuous success. By main strength and awkwardness I managed to clamber up. Just as I reached the top and put my rifle down, so that as I panted I might fan breath into myself with both hands, my boot soles slipped on the uncertain surface and I slid off my perch into space. Wildly I threw out both arms in a northerly direction. My clutching fingers closed on a limb of a maple, which overshadowed the rock, and I swung out into the air twelve feet or so above the inhospitable earth and utterly unable to reach with my convulsively groping feet the nearermost jut of granite. For an agonized moment it seemed probable that the only thing that I might break my fall with would be myself. But I kept my presence of mind. I flatter myself that in emergencies I am a quick thinker. As I dangled there an expedient came to me. I let go gradually.

And then as I plumped with a dull sickening thud into the herbage below and lay there weaponless, windless and jarred, I saw vanishing into the scrub not a hundred feet away the black shape of a big and startled moose. I caught one fleeting glimpse of an enormous head, of a profile which might have belonged to one of the Major Prophets, of a set of horns outspreading even as the fronded palm outspreads itself, of a switching tail and a slab-sided rump, and then the shielding bushes closed and the apparition was gone, and gone for keeps. For my part there was nothing to do but to sit there for a spell and cherish regrets. Under the circumstances, trailing a frightened bull moose would have been about as satisfactory as trailing a comet, and probably not a bit more successful as to results.

For the majority of the members of our troupe the duration of the hunt had a time limit. On the afternoon of the last day in camp, two of the party strolled into the immediate presence of a fair-sized bull and firing together, one of them put a slug of lead in a twitching ear which he turned toward them. It must have been his deaf ear, else he would have been aware of their approach long before. But one moose was singular and the achievement of the plural number was our ambition. So four of us crossed back into New Brunswick, where according to all native New Brunswickers the moose grow larger than they do in the sister province, Nova Scotians taking the opposite side and being willing to argue it at all times.

With unabated determination the gallant quartet of us hunted and hunted. Three big deer died to make holiday for us, but the moose displayed a coyness and diffidence which might be accounted for only on the ground that they had heard we were coming. Indeed they could not very well help hearing it.

Each morning under the influences of the frost the flaming forest colors showed a dimming hue. Day before yesterday they had been like burning brands, yesterday there were dulled embers, to-day smoldering coals; and tomorrow they would be as dead ashes. Each night the sun went down in a nimbus of cold gray clouds. There was a taste and a smell as of snow in the air. The last tardy robin packed up and went south; the swarms of juncoes grew thicker; wedge-shaped flights of coot and black duck passed overhead, their bills all pointing toward the Gulf of Mexico. Then on the last day there fell a rain which turned to sleet and the sleet in turn to snow—four inches of it—and in the snow on that last day the reward which comes—some-times—to the persevering was ours.

To know the climactic sensation which filled the triumphant ama-teur you must first of all care for the outdoors and for big game shooting, and in the second place you must have known the feeling of hope deferred, and in the third place you must have reached the eleventh hour, so to speak, of your stay in these parts with the antici-pation you had been nurturing for all these weeks since the trip was first proposed, still unrealized in your soul.

You and your camp mate and your guide were on the last lap of the journey back to camp; the sun was slipping down the western wall of the horizon; the shadows were deepening under the spruces; you rounded the shoulder of a ridge and stood for a moment at your guide's back looking out across a fire-burned barren. He stiffened like a pointer on a warm scent and pointed straight ahead. Your eye fol-lowed where his finger aimed, and two hundred yards away you saw a dark blot against a background of faded tamarack—a bull standing head-on. You shot together, you and your companion. Apparently unscathed, the animal swung himself about and started moving at the seemingly languid lope of the moose, which really is a faster gait than you would suppose until you measure the length of his stride. You kept on firing, both of you, as rapidly almost as you could pull the triggers of your automatics. Twice he shook himself and humped his hind-quarters as though stung, but he did not check his speed. You emptied your magazine—five shots. Your mate's fifth shell jammed in the chamber, putting him out of the running for the moment. In desperate haste you fumbled one more shell into your rifle, and just as the fugitive topped a little rise before disappearing for good into the shrouding second-growth, you got your sight full on the mark and sent a farewell bullet whistling on its way. The black hulk vanished magically.

"That'll do," said your guide, grinning broadly, "you got 'im. But load up again before we go over there. He's down and down for keeps, I think, judgin' by the way he flopped, but he might get up again."

But he didn't get up again. You came on him where he lay, still feebly twitching, with two flesh wounds in his flanks and a third hole right through him behind the shoulders—a thousand pounds of meat, a head worth saving and mounting and bragging about in the years to come, a pelt as big as a double blanket and at last the accomplished plural of moose was mise.

CHAPTER 3

MARY STANLEY BRECK

wife of noted American sportsman Eddie Breck, 1925

THE LADY & THE MOOSE: A LETTER

Dear Queenie:

In your last letter, written just as Eddie and I were starting for the tangled timber and the yellow moose-bogs, you say, "I never thought that you would go hunting for anything. Did you go and did you see a moose? I am sure I would run the other way if I saw one coming!"

Well, I've been and gone and done it, though I admit that I never suspected myself capable, either ethically or sportively, of hunting anything, at least anything with warm blood, for you know I am a brazen and unregenerate fisherwoman. It all came about like this. Eddie is one of those men who, though they pretend to allow us women our place in the sun, yet, way down in their subconscious minds, they fancy themselves just a wee bit superior to us in some ways, and one of my objects in life is to show him—you understand. So when I rather scoffed at moose-hunting, and he remarked that possibly it was a sport rather for the strong, masculine nature rather than the weaker feminine, and all that, my entire femininity rose in revolt and I announced that I was to be one of the party, and that I would do my full share of lugging and other hardships. I rather think Eddie was a little surprised, both at my decision and the fitness of my preparations.

I am sending you a photograph of myself in hunting togs. It looks all right on the outside, but don't think I have put on half a ton in weight. It is only that Eddie insisted that I wear wool next to my skin, and, what with things of that kind, including a heavy, high-necked and long-sleeved undershirt (one of his) and two pairs of wool stockings in hunting-shoes (also his), I felt at first like a stuffed porker. However, I got used to it, and Eddie was right. The north woods in October, except in the full sunshine, are not exactly like the Willard on a ball night. I carried my only weapon slung over my shoulder. Don't be alarmed. It wasn't a gun but a camera. I did have a little .22 rifle, but had no intention of imbuing my hands in blood. I was simply the official photographer, and this letter is to tell you how efficiently I accomplished my mission.

Eddie's old traditional hunting-ground was on Silver Lake. But that seemed a long way to drag one's wife through the wilderness, so we concluded to choose the vicinity of Elder Lake [Annapolis

*A lady and her moose.
Pictured is Josephine Lovett,
wife of Dr. Lewis Lovett,
Bear River, who was doctor
for the village and surrounding districts from 1892 to
1942. Both were avid
hunters and anglers. Unlike
Mrs. Breck, she bagged this
moose—her first—with a gun.*

County], only about two hours' journey by canoe and portage, and, in order to pre-empt the territory, we had made camp on the other side of Elder (two lean-tos and a big fly), and moved over most of our provisions the week before the season opened.

It was a lovely, calm day when we started, and the lake mirrored the brilliant colors of the Nova Scotia autumn lusciously. A touch of soberness was added by the great, gray, granite rocks that stand picturesquely along the banks and often in the lake itself. There had been nearly a fortnight of wonderful mornings for moose-calling, namely, calm and cold, even frosty, with a filmy mist on the water which rose and floated away gently as the sun smiled through it. If only this weather would continue for another week, our bull moose was as good as bagged!

I must admit that I was astonished when I saw the loads the men toted over the carriers, and I marveled when I reflected that a certain one of the party, now bending under a load of bedding and a heavy pack-basket, was prone to groan when he was asked, in Washington, D. C., to carry a travel-ing-bag down to the car. As for Ritson, (our guide), a giant in build, he placed a fifty-pound load on his back and then set the canoe atop of all, grabbed his ax and rifle, and walked off as if he were giving his baby girl a ride. The portage itself, or carry, as they call it in Nova Scotia, was not so bad, except when the trail led through a soft, wet bog, or up a steep incline. Then I appreciated the fact that we who habitually walk on the level plaster use few of our muscles, and walk on our heels more than toes.

Eddie pointed out a lusty young fir, which had been badly battered, in fact broken in two, by a bull moose slashing with his antlers, either for battle practice, or, as some say, to rub the velvet off. In any case it meant the near presence of the quarry and greatly heartened us, for we had begun to despair on account of the absence of fresh tracks and other "signs" of the game we were after.

American sportsman Eddie Breck, left, with his Milford guide Ritson Longmire, "a giant in build."

The location of our *permanent* camp was both delightful and cozy. Though within thirty yards of the landing, the opening with the tents was hardly visible from the lake. The two tents were set up nearly beside one another and the dining-fly opposite, the fireplace being between. Under the fly was an improvised but convenient table of boards brought from an abandoned lumber camp near-by. The men had the whole thing done in very quick time, and I felt as though I should like to stay there for weeks, so cozy and homelike it was. Since then I have laughed to myself at the term permanent camp, for out of seven days we stayed there just two nights, though we returned during the daytime nearly always. In the "calling" season it is the custom to establish a fixed home like ours, as a head-quarters, but to spend the nights at or near the places where the calling is to be done. A tent and enough food for night and morning meals are taken along, plus bedding, and a bivouac made for the night only.

I must confess that I felt somewhat *de trop,* not to say a bit piqued at the way in which the men started in to cook without asking me to help, in fact without apparently taking any notice of me at all. And you know how I pride myself on my cooking at home, of course when I don't really have to. However, later on they did graciously allow me to do certain menial duties, such as making the coffee. As to the food itself, candor compels me to acknowledge that it was excellent, even the Johnnie-cake, baked in the reflector before the fire. When I look back though, I rather think that one great reason for its excellence was that appetite "that mother used to make" or the strenuous outdoor life.

I must confess that I felt somewhat de trop, *not to say a bit piqued at the way in which the men started in to cook without asking me to help, in fact without apparently taking any notice of me at all.*

There is something very like ceremony in the last preparations for a moose-hunt. You feel it in the air. Your mind is concentrated on the weather conditions and you find yourself scanning the sky every few minutes. However, I am not going to tell you about the times when the conditions were not right. There were two occasions when we went out and started to hunt, but had to give it up, and returned to camp. It had been decided that, since a woman cannot very well negotiate the killing swamps and jungles which must be covered in still-hunting, and because Eddie wanted me to "see how it was done," we should do no tramping after moose, which he calls "still-hunting in calling time," but should confine ourselves to calling. Since the Nova Scotia law allows shooting only on the first of October, calling is not so easy as it was when the season began on September 15, the time when the moose start to mate, and when, on that account, the big bulls can still be interested. By October the big fellows have all secured their mates, leaving only the smaller bulls as bachelors. This is the reason why such a lot of small ones come to the call. If a big one is wanted, recourse must actually be had to still-hunting, which is done at this season by tracking the mated pairs and approaching them while sounding the bull call, as well as that of the cow, through the birchen horn, the bull usually resenting the interference of a rival, until the quarry is sighted. Moose-calling, as every hunter knows, is one of the most picturesque practices of the woods.

Eddie was not optimistic about our hunt. He had been so successful in times past that he was prepared for a failure this year. Besides, as he put it, when you want to show off before your wife, and pose as one of those noble denizens of the "big, wide spaces, where a man's a man," you usually get beautifully left. Then there was the lack of fresh signs, and the evident change to unfavorable weather. It was, therefore, without any very high hopes that we made our way up the lovely lake on the afternoon of the sixth, each tree a flaming torch, crossed the height of land to the eastward, and made our bivouac for the night near Little Sunrise Lake, in a perfect tangle of brush, which had literally to be cut out to accommodate the tent. No wood was cut, as there might be a moose near-by, but dry stuff was collected and a small fire made almost at our feet, as we lay in our sleeping-bags into which we crept, almost as soon as the sun went down when the cold damp of the evening crept upon us.

We had had but one good opportunity for calling, but that had been of an evening and Eddie had only called a few times and very softly, as he did not believe in shooting in any but full daylight. In this he differed from most of the guides, who assert that the bull will come more readily in the evening. But Eddie had had some sour experiences, as had many of his acquaintances. I remember his telling of a moose shot at in the dusk that had got away wounded and suffering. I agree with Eddie. It is unsportsmanlike to shoot at anything one is not sure of killing at once.

One does not always sleep quietly in the woods. The conditions are unusual. There are eerie sounds from beyond that narrow camp-fire radius, from the great Stygian blackness. The barred owls are very vocal, and there was one at Sunrise that night that hadn't learned to call right, or else he stuttered. Anyhow we got to laughing at him and that kept us awake. When we did doze off, we continually awoke to consult our watch. The first time I was sure we had slept too late, but it was only midnight! And then two, and then three. And then I felt a gentle shake at my shoulder and heard a faint

No device for wooing sleep could excel the regulation forest bed of fragrant fir-boughs, into which tired limbs sink gratefully. No kitchen can look half so cheery as the row of pothooks hung over the ruddy glow of sparkling birch logs, especially when the air is fragrant with 'the something hot' preparing for the usual toast, 'Here's luck to-morrow,' that winds up the camp-fire yarns.

Arthur Silver, 1907

crackle from the fire which gave the only light there was. It was Eddie, who had gathered the almost dead embers and hung the coffee pot over the small blaze in the midst of the blackness.

"Four o'clock," he said in a low voice. "Better get up and put on everything you've got. You can see the stars through the tree-tops. It's perfect weather. I'll call Ritson." The guide was bunking under a tarpaulin not far away and was soon with us, trying to keep warm at the tiny fire, for it was bitter cold. We spoke in whispers, for there might be a moose near-by—the bulls travel at this time of year, looking for mates, those who are yet unmarried. But there was an exhilaration in our hearts hard to describe. We all radiated optimism. The hot coffee and the doughnuts merely added to our content, and it took us only a short time to complete our hunting toilette and possess ourselves of the needed equipment: Eddie, his rifle and "call," Ritson, the lantern and the navy blanket in which I was to wrap myself, and I with the camera. Quickly, though gingerly, we felt our way in the dark over the rough path to the lake, a quarter of a mile away, all bathed in a

filmy, mysterious mist through which we paddled slowly, so as not to collide with the ever-present rocks so prevalent in that country. By dead reckoning we arrived at the further shore, which was the edge of a bog some hundred yards in extent, where the canoe was drawn up in the hardhacks, while we listened from time to time for the call of a moose. But, except the far-off cry of an owl, all was silence. We threaded our slow, wet way across the bog, and up a slight ascent, keeping the swamp on our right, until at last we came to the bog where Eddie intended to call. It was some two hundred yards long and less than that broad, and we took our stations at a rock near the southern end, as moose usually appeared at the northern end, from the wild country beyond. Eddie stopped at the edge of the bog, motioned us to silence, and, kneeling down, pointed his horn at the ground and emitted a most lugubrious, heartbroken, whining bellow, not very loud. This was on the chance that there might be a bull in the near vicinity. It is impossible to describe this woe-begone call of the cow moose in love. It must certainly be heard to be fully appreciated. I am unable to say how well my lord and master (as they said in the Victorian age) imitates her ladyship of the forest, but, in view of what followed, I should say sufficiently well.

Strange and uncanny is the complete, dead silence which immediately follows a loud sound in the dead calm of a frosty morning. Then there seems to come a rushing of all sorts of noises, no doubt most imaginary, among which one recognizes the ticking of one's watch and especially the beating of one's heart, which makes so much noise that it seems impossible to listen to anything else. Here on Sunrise Lake bog there was yet another source of sound, about which I had not been told beforehand, and which somewhat confused me when I tried to recognize the answer of the bull as described to me. It was the hardly, yet clearly, audible rushing of a waterfall some two miles off to the north.

There was apparently no answer to Eddie's low call, and in about ten minutes he raised the horn again and sent a long, loud, quavering, yearning cry into the air, so that it reverberated over the hemlocks and pines like the rolling of a cannon boom. Hardly had he dropped the call from his mouth when far off to the southeast a dog barked. I wondered that a dog could be heard so far off, even on this still morning, as there was no house within many miles of us. But the two men glanced at each other meaningly, and then Eddie arched his eyebrows at me, evidently registering inquiry. I stared back vacantly.

"Hear that?" he whispered. "A bull!"

I looked, "Oh!" but said nothing, though I could see no reason for keeping so still when the bull was miles away; but it had been impressed upon me that, on the calling-ground, the penalty of the slightest sound, and still more the slightest movement, was sudden death, so I merely listened. My heart started to beat harder, for the great animal, the rendezvous with which had been so long and carefully planned, with the experience and acquired skill of a lifetime, was actually off there in the thick forest! He had heard us, and was coming to the tryst, for him the tryst of death!

The next twenty minutes or so were exciting, though I could hear nothing suspicious, though the men said he was coming steadily. As we stood, or rather sat, there like statues, the rising sun began to color the sky, and then the alders and hackmatacks from which the mist floated off into the air. The bushes dripped dew, and here and there a sparrow fluttered out, and suddenly the bog seemed alive with yellow points of light which were really millions of white millers, not one of which seemed to find a place to alight, but kept continuously on the wing. So fascinated was I with this strange and beautiful spectacle that I started when Eddie whispered, with a warning gesture, "Get down—he's right over there!"

In a moment I, too, heard a kind of swishing in the bushes, so near that my heart was in my mouth. The two men were evidently worried, and I thought I understood their anxiety. The bull had approached to within a hundred yards or so, and was evidently working around us. In a few moments he might cross our trail, get our scent, and then "Good-bye, Sir Moose!"

Eddie and Ritson stuck their heads close together. Eddie nodded and softly knelt down and placed the big end of his call almost against the wet earth. An agonized, yearning, hoarse whine sounded over the bog. I have been told since that this was the great test of skill in the calling art. Almost any sound will start a bull a long way off, but to deceive one only eighty or a hundred yards distant—another matter! It was, in this case, sheer desperation, for unless stopped the bull was lost to us.

The instants following this last appeal of Eddie's were anxious and exciting to the point of torture. Were we to be disappointed after all, when the bull had come so beautifully and regularly? Why didn't the men make a dash in the direction of the bull? We knew almost exactly where he must be, and they might get a shot at close quarters. But Eddie preferred to trust to his skill. At his last call the bull had ceased speaking, and there was absolute silence. What would happen? Would we suddenly hear a panicky rush through the thicket, and then—nothing more?

Eddie Breck with the fruits of his labour. Breck was one of the original non-resident sportsman to come to Nova Scotia and spent many years extolling the virtues of our woods and waters to fellow Americans through his writings in sporting magazines and books.

Suddenly Ritson made an almost imperceptible movement with his head and Eddie slowly raised his rifle. Seventy yards to our right a big, black head, with yellow, sweeping antlers, was poised in the mass of alders and maples. [For] a second the beast seemed to gaze straight at us, and then slowly and deliberately the great animal walked out on the open bog, huge, black, ungainly!

About fifty feet from where he emerged he stopped and stood, almost broadside on, looking at us. As Eddie glanced steadily along his rifle, I knew that great, magnificent beast was gone, and it seemed as if I should cry out, "No—don't kill him!" And then I thought of the camera in my shaking hands, and that my duty was to get a good picture. I vaguely thought, "There he is, and the light is fine, and I must get him quickly!"

I did get the camera up, though I could not take my eyes off the great black bull, but just as I was nerving myself to focus him, "Bang!" went Eddie's rifle. I don't know what I did, probably nothing at all but gasp, as the great animal turned from us and trotted across the bog. "Bang!" again, and then once more. Eddie says that he fired all the cartridges in his rifle, five. I could not begin to say. I only watched the bull as he fled. Could it be possible that Eddie had missed him at that distance, and in that light? No—he is wobbling! He is badly hit! There—he's down. Thank God! Oh, I never want to see anything killed again!

Hysterically (I was hysterical, anyhow!) we made our difficult way across the wet, soft bog. We could not see the bull until we were on the other side, but at last we stood beside him. He was stone-dead, and, fortunately, literally never knew what struck him, as could be seen by the photograph that we took of his heart, through the middle of which Eddie's bullet, no doubt the first one he fired, had passed. I could not understand how a beast could run over a hundred yards with a bullet through his heart, but Eddie assures me that it is a common occurrence.

It was not until a half-hour later, as we were about to re-enter the canoe to paddle back to camp, that Eddie suddenly caught me by the arm and asked, "Oh, Mimi, did you get the photograph?"

"I—I—don't exactly know!" I replied. "Perhaps!"

But, dear Queenie, I didn't!

CHAPTER 4

CAMPBELL
HARDY
British army
officer, Halifax,
1853

A Winter Hunt

"Mornin, Sir! splendid day for huntin, this! Plenty wind, and snow beautiful soft. Like to be in the woods away to the eastward this mornin, Sir, along with you," said the Indian Williams, one of the best hunters in the province, as he marched into my room [at the British garrison in Halifax] one tolerably sharp morning towards the end of February, in the year 1853.

"Ah, Williams, is that you?" said I to the copper-coloured denizen of the woods, who had squatted himself down with his back towards me, over the fire, and was drawing volumes of not very savoury tobacco smoke from the bowl of an old black pipe, with the least possible particle of stem appertaining to it.

"Yes, Capting, I was out along with gentleman, other day, away to Musquedoboit, between there and Ship Harbour Lake, and saw—my sakes!—I never see such lot of tracks—ground reglar tramped up by moose. Startin five moose day before yesterday but only see small piece of one as he go off through the bushes. Bad luck, and bad sort of weather. S'pose you go, Capting, and we have tolerable weather, you fire all day, I promise you."

"Well, Williams, I've a good mind to go out with you for a week or ten days. Do you think I shall bring back moose meat?"

"Sartin, Capting, ten days plenty—s'pose we come back empty-handed—that is if you shoot well, and no miss every time, as some gentleman does, I give you five dollars, and you no pay me nothin for my huntin."

"Done with you, Williams," said I. "I'll go and get someone to join me, and you must procure another Indian hunter, and a boy to keep camp; and mind, we will start from here at three o'clock this afternoon so as to get a good piece along the road to-night, and arrive at our hunting grounds, and fix camp before dark to-morrow."

I have invariably found that an excursion into the woods, of long or short duration, is sure to prove more enjoyable, if got up on the spur of the moment. If you make up your mind long before it comes off, you have most likely in your reveries and dreams forestalled the excitement of your sport. And then again, on an excursion quickly settled, you start in favourable weather, which will most probably attend you for the first two or three days at least. And the finding yourself too, wrapped up in the old homespun coat, still redolent of the fragrant spruce boughs, on which you reclined in your last trip into the bush, trudging away under your load of blankets, on the same day that you had been looking idly out your window, comes with additional, unexpected pleasure.

I was not long in finding a companion, or in packing up the necessary number of blankets, axes, guns, and the prog, the procuring and amount of which had been left to me, as being an old hand at such matters. On the present occasion, as there would be five hungry mouths to feed for more than a week, we laid in a stock consisting of thirty pounds of fat pork, wherewithal to fry our moose-meat, or whatever other spoil our guns might procure us; fifty pounds of hard biscuit, tea, sugar, some tobacco for ourselves and plenty of an inferior description for the Indians, whose zeal in your service would wonderfully flag if their calumets were not well supplied with the fragrant weed. The necessary condiments, pepper and salt, with a good supply of onions, barley, rice, and peas, as ingredients for our soup-kettle, completed our commissariat arrangements.

Campbell Hardy's Micmac guide, John Williams, standing next to John Thomas (Paddy) Lane of Halifax custom-house. Williams wears the hunting knife presented to him by Prince Arthur in September 1869.

Most of these were rolled up in one of the blankets, while the remainder, and the old camp-kettle, a sort of nest of pots and pans,

knives and forks, all fitting snugly one within another, a most inge-
nious and indispensable contrivance for the woods, were enveloped
in another. Of course, an absurd number of bullets are generally
taken on a hunting expedition, sufficient to exterminate the moose in
the district fixed upon as the hunting grounds. However, it is as well
to take enough, as, if you have a bad day, the unfitness of which for
hunting entails stopping at home, shooting at a mark outside the
camp becomes a favourite amusement both with yourselves and the
Indians.

It was rather late in the afternoon when a well-furred sleigh and
pair drove up, and the loading process commenced—an operation
which was performed carefully, as the depth of the snow, and the
unbeaten state of the roads, at some distance from the town, would

Sport Martin Rosenburg strikes a pose beside an assortment of gear and trappings, Chezzetcook, Halifax County, ca. 1899.

entail a considerable amount of jolting. Everything having been stowed away snugly underneath, except the guns, which should never be allowed to leave one's hands, the Indian jumped in behind, and my companion taking the ribands, with a "Let her go! Go lang, you hosses!" we glided away down the steep streets of Halifax, rattling on board of the steam ferry boat, which conveys passengers and sleighs, or waggons, from Halifax to the pretty little town of Dartmouth, on the opposite side of the harbour.

Ten minutes steaming, a short drag up a rather precipitous hill in Dartmouth, and a few more spent in passing the suburbs, and we were trotting out on a well-beaten level road by the side of a chain of lakes, which, commencing about half a mile from the town, stretch away to the north-west for about twenty miles, and give rise to the river Shubenacadie, the river of Acadia, which empties itself into the basin of Minas. It was a glorious evening, and, though intense frost prevailed, the calmness of the air diminished its effect upon our noses. The moon had just risen, and somewhat "paled the ineffectual fires" of a splendid aurora. The going was beautiful. The light sleigh glided over the frozen snow with an almost imperceptible motion, its runners, as they cut through the crisp surface, causing that peculiar crackling sound, always heard when the sleighing is good. The jingling of the merry bells attached to the horse collars, our lighted pipes, our feeling of comparative comfort, as we regarded the cold and desolate forest scenery from beneath our ample buffalo robes, all conduced to keep us in the highest spirits.

Then the visions of moose—huge animals standing to be shot at in gloomy recesses of the woods, mixed up with, in a confused manner, those of Indians, lucifees, porcupines, huge wood fires, and savoury messes in camp, flitted across our fancies, and made us long for the completion of our journey. A couple of hours more, however, made a great change in our mettle, if not in that of our animals. The cold contracted sensation in our hands and faces, made the fifteen-mile house, where we baited ourselves and horses, a very desirable refuge for a quarter of an hour.

A few miles farther on, we stopped for the night; and after a deal of hammering at all the doors and windows of an old wooden house, succeeded in inducing the Bluenose proprietor to give us the key of his stable, and to set his daughters to work at blowing up the embers of the kitchen fire, and broiling thereon the everylasting ham and eggs, which are set before the traveller at every meal in the roadside inns of Nova Scotia. Another hour, and the whole party were snoring in concert, under the unrolled blankets, on the plank floor of the kitchen.

February 28: We were aroused this morning by Williams' tolerably loud observation of, "Most time to be thinkin of startin, gentlemen. I tink he's going to be some sort of weather this mornin. He look very dark to southward. I 'most 'fraid soft weather comin. Better be startin soon, while snow good."

Jumping up and giving ourselves a hearty shake, we went blinking into the open air. It did look like a change, and in Nova Scotia, changes follow each other fast and furious. After breakfast, which consisted of ham and eggs again of course, with pickles and cheese, the horses were put to, and we spun along to the tune of the bells, the drag, however, being heavier this morning from the softened state of the snow. From the tops of hills we obtained some fine glimpses of the dark expansive forest, and of the numerous frozen lakes, which

Camp between Lake Jolly and Ninth Lake, Digby County, ca. 1890s. L-R: Bear River Micmac guide Malti Pictou, two unidentified sports, Micmac guide John Labrador, junior guide and 'campkeeper' Louis Peters.

lay in its bosom, covered with a smooth mantle of snow.

A couple of hours took us over the Red Bridge, on the Musquedoboit River, which was blocked up nearly to the top of its steep banks by masses of ice. Avoiding the settlement of Middle Musquedoboit, we took the small road to the eastward, which in another hour brought us to the last house in that direction, where we were to leave our sleigh, and regularly take to the bush. Williams here went off to an Indian camp, about half a mile distant, for the purpose of engaging another Indian hunter, and a boy, to keep camp, while we turned in to the house, and enjoyed our last meal, for some time, under a roof.

The two Indians, whom Williams had engaged for us, soon made their appearance, evidently eager for the job. They were father and son, old Francis Paul, the father, being a remarkably athletic looking Indian, and thoroughly acquainted with the country and habits of the moose round Ship Harbour, as was afterwards proved. His son Joe undertook the office of camp-keeper, whose business is to cut wood for the camp-fire, to act as cook, to pick fresh beds of boughs at least twice a week, and do anything that be required in the neighbourhood of the camp.

"Couldn't have come no better time, Sir, nor to no better country. Plenty moose, and beautiful country for creepin," said old Paul, as we sallied forth from the house, following a small sled, drawn by the set-tler's pony, which was to convey our luggage as far as practicable.

"Well, Paul, I'm glad to hear it. How far have we to go to-night, to camp?"

"'Bout eight mile, Capting. I've got old camp at this end of big lake, where I tink we stop to-night, and hunt country round, to-morrow. Then, next day, we go on to Fish Lake for good."

To which arrangement we having assented, a long dialogue com-menced between Williams and the two other Indians, in their own melodious and soft language, during which I distinguished the words, *teeam* (moose), and *caribou* (Anglice, reindeer), very frequently. The language of an Indian dialogue is harmonious in more than one sense, since they all seem to acknowledge the truth of each other's remarks, by the frequent use of the word "Eh-hé," or, "yes, exactly so." The Micmac dialect is by far the finest of the many spoken by the various tribes which inhabit North America, and is very widely circulated through the provinces of Nova Scotia, New Brunswick, and part of Canada. Few white men understand more than a few casual words.

It was a dreadfully broken and rocky road, and, for a long distance, ran through an elevated country, covered with burnt woods, and sprinkled with immense boulders of granite. The old sled cracked and grated over the rocky strata, here and there denuded of snow by the wind. Before we had proceeded a mile, we saw the Indians, who were chatting away merrily in front, stop and gaze at something on the ground, pointing towards some distant barrens, which were visible on the right. It was the track of a caribou, which, they said, had crossed the road the day previously. The remainder of the journey was down hill, the path very contracted, and overhung by the long arms of the hemlocks, and, in some places, there was scarcely room between the trees for the sled to pass.

Canoes and wagons were a more common means of conveyance to the sporting grounds than sleighs and snowshoes. Winter hunts were enjoyed principally by the British officers in the mid-1800s as laws were changed by the latter part of the century, imposing shortened autumn seasons as well as smaller bag limits and occasional moratoriums to protect the endangered caribou and moose.

Several more tracks of caribou, of different ages, and those of two moose, which had been there not many hours before us, were passed, before arriving at the edge of a lake, where the path ended, and we had to take to the ice. Joe, going on, and making two or three incisions with his axe, pronounced the ice to be perfectly safe, and we led the pony and sled on to the lake. The travelling was now easy, and we jumped up on the top of the luggage, and our animal mustering up a trot, we were speedily transported to the other end of the lake, about four miles distant from where we had entered it.

Here the conveyance was dismissed, and the Indians adjusted the baggage into suitable loads of about fifty pounds weight each, carrying them in the blankets, the ends of which turned inwards, were drawn up by a broad leather band, which bears on the chest and shoulders. The blanket thus fashioned according to the Indian plan, becomes a complete bag, out of which nothing can slip. It rests on the back over the shoulders, and does not project beyond them, as it would then catch against the stems of trees in travelling through thick bush, and impede the progress of the bearer.

There was only an hour's daylight to be calculated upon, when, after trudging under our loads through a swampy piece of ground, into which we sunk every now and then up to our knees, we arrived at Paul's old camp, by the side of Ship Harbour Lake. No time could be spared, for the camp wanted a good deal of *fixin*. Beds had to be picked and arranged, firewood cut, and a mass of snow, which had fallen in through the top of the camp, shovelled out. However, five hands all used to it soon made things appear comfortable, and, at the expiration of the hour, we were sitting on an ample and fragrant bed of the tender boughs of the silver fir, in front of a huge pile of blazing logs. We lit our pipes—the hunter's solace after fatigue, when a spare moment occurs—and looked with much satisfaction upon the great frying-pan filled with noisy slices of pork hissing over the flames. In the mean-while, the tea-kettle being removed spluttering from the fire, informed us that operations might be commenced by a cup of the beverage "which cheers, but not inebriates."

Balmy sleep soon after the meal overtook the inhabitants of the camp, interrupted however, suddenly, about the middle of the night, by a most appalling crash close to the camp, which at once awoke us. It was blowing a furious gale right up the lake, and the rain rattled against the bark-covered side of our camp.

"What was that horrid row outside, just now?" I asked of the half-awakened Indians.

"Sartin, Capting, big tree fall close to camp."

And they were right, for at daylight next morning, we found that the trunk of dead pine had fallen during the night, missing our camp by a couple of yards.

February 29: The prospect was dismal, and the rain still falling when we emerged from under our shanty this morning. The old ice on the lake, which stretched away as far as we could see, till it and its lofty wooded banks were lost in the drizzling mist, was covered by nearly six inches of water. The snow had nearly disappeared from the ground round our camp, the bottom of which was saturated with water, though our beds were, fortunately, dry from their having been raised on layers of wood. A few hundred yards below the camp, the Gaspereau River, swollen to twice its usual size, fell roaring into the lake, rendering the ice broken and insecure for some distance around its mouth.

"Bad day for huntin," said old Paul. "I tink, however, some snow left still in the woods, and no tellin, might be moose handy."

"Well Paul, let's go in out of the wet and get breakfast, and then we will talk about what's to be done!"

Joe had turned the course of the water, which had been flowing regularly through our camp, by a circular trench, and, opening an old cellar constructed on a hill-side, had extracted there, from a basket of

fine potatoes and dried smelts, which latter had been taken in the lake during the past summer.

This morning, our stay in camp was longer than is usually the case, as little was expected to be done during the day in the woods, and old Paul diverted us with some anecdotes of the hunting he had enjoyed at different times in this neighbourhood. The camp we were now in was his summer and fall residence, and was built on ground granted by Government to the Indians, called the Indian reserve. A capital location this appeared to be for an Indian wigwam. The adjacent woods are full of moose, porcupine, and hares. The Big Lake, a stone's-throw from the camp, was seventeen miles in length, and connected with the Atlantic at its lower extremity by a short arm. In the summer months, it teems with salmon, fresh-water and sea trout, smelts and gaspereaux, which two latter fish are to be taken in great quantities in the river below the camp. Paul informed us that, last fall, he had shot, in the neighbouring forest, two moose and a caribou, and had put up more than a dozen barrels of gaspereaux and smelts, which he had disposed of advantageously at the settlement, twelve miles distant.

After a long smoke, we agreed to start, so, loading the guns, anointing both the outside of the barrels, and the finger-ends of kid-gloves, in which the bullets were sewn up and rammed down, plentifully with mercurial ointment, we sallied forth. Sheets of birch-bark rolled up into cones were placed over the hammers to protect them and the nipples from damp, and could be slipped off immediately in case of need. As the hunting country lay on the other side of the river, which it was impracticable to cross at this point, we were forced to make a long detour on the lake. The water on the surface penetrated through moccasins and socks at the first step, and struck bitterly cold to the feet, while the surface of the ice underneath was so slippery that it was hard to avoid falling at every step, but a few minutes' tramp through the woods sufficed to restore circulation to our benumbed feet.

The country was very hilly, the tops of the hills covered with hard-wood and apparently holding forth great inducements from the thickets of young shrubs for moose to frequent them as feeding grounds, while their sides, covered with tall hemlocks and pines and the mossy swamps at their feet, appeared likely retreats for these animals during their hours of repose. Strange to say, we did not see a single sign of moose having recently been anywhere in the broad tract of forest which we traversed—not a single track. We arrived at our camp about dusk, rather discomfited, and wet to the skin. However, lighting our pipes, after a hearty meal on soup and biscuits, our troubles were soon forgotten.

Breakfast on the trail at 'Dominical Camp,' Little Dish Lake Stream, ca. 1890s. Note the sports-man's umbrella hanging from the tree in centre fore-ground.

"Well, what's the reason we have not seen a moose track to-day, Paul? I suppose you scared them all away the last time you were down here."

"Well, Capting, I didn't much think we find um here—too much hunted round here last fall by settler and brutes of dogs—only I thought might be as well to try. 'Morrow we move off to other camp, away back to Fish Lake, where I know moose shocking plenty."

Our clothes were soon dry, and stretching out on the boughs in front of the blazing billets, we soon fell asleep.

On the first of March, there was a glorious change in the weather. We awoke, and found flakes of snow falling into the camp through the aperture in the top, which served as an egress for the smoke. We all went outside at once, and found the scene completely changed by the light and airy effect, which always accompanies a fresh fall of snow in the woods. Every spray of the boughs was coated with fresh snow, the dazzling whiteness of which caused the depths of the woods to lose their gloom, and the perspective of the forest scenery to be materially altered. About two inches had fallen—quite enough for creeping.

"Wish we were at other lake this mornin, we most sure to have moose-steak for dinner to-night."

"Well, let's get breakfast, make up the loads, and start at once," we both exclaimed.

"What's Williams about there on the lake?"

"He catchin smelt," said Paul, "I tole him to get some for breakfast."

Delicious little fish they were, as was provided at breakfast. Williams had caught two dozen of them in as many minutes, with a small hook baited with a piece of pork, through a hole in the ice.

Directly after breakfast, the Indians making up and shouldering the loads upon their backs, followed by us carrying our blankets and guns, started for a tramp of eight miles through the bush to another large lake, which gave rise to the Gaspereau River, and round the shores of which we were to hunt for the remainder of our ten days.

The snow still continued to fall, a cold shower often descending on our necks as our heads brushed against the heavily laden branches of the firs. We passed through every variety of bush, by far the most pleasant for travelling being the tall greenwoods composed of hemlocks and pines, with very little underwood to impede our progress. The hard-woods were dreadful. Fallen trees lay about in all directions, inflicting frequent bruises on our feet and ankles, while the frozen boughs of the thickets of young wood, through which we had to force our way, often gave us sharp cuts across the face, forcing out many an exclamation of impatience.

The swamps not being yet sufficiently frozen to bear one everywhere, now and then let us down above our ankles in the soft moss, which distilled bitterly cold water into our moccasins. Three hours hard trudging through the woods, and over numerous small lakes and extensive caribou barrens, (as the plains of Nova Scotia, covered with soft mosses and lichens of every description, are called, from their being the grounds of the American reindeer), brought us out on the banks of the Gaspereau River, about two miles from Fish Lake—our destination.

We crossed the river by a natural bridge formed of the trunk of a lofty beech, which had fallen over the channel. It is interesting to watch the steadiness with which an Indian, under an enormous load, will walk along any trunk or branch that will bear him. Their feet, not stiffened by constant enclosure within a hard casing like our leather boots and shoes, possess the same muscular power of grasping as those of a monkey.

My companion and the other Indians had gone ahead, when old Paul found and showed me fresh tracks of three moose, which had been passed unnoticed by the others.

Men of fame and fortune were drawn to Nova Scotia in the halcyon days of hunting and fishing—doctors, lawyers, politicians, railroad presidents, financiers, professional athletes, corporate executives—men with surnames like Rockefeller and Roosevelt. Many stayed in camps no better than the one pictured here. Yet they never complained, unlike the average sport of the post World War II era, who demanded "the best for the least."

"Quite fresh, Sir, only this mornin'," whispered he, putting down his bundle. "Your gun loaded, Sir? I tink we creep for few minutes."

"All right Paul," said I, putting on caps, and following the Indian, who was now gliding cautiously through the bush, regarding with scrutiny the various signs of the vicinity of moose. The red juicy tops of the young maples had been freshly bitten off, sometimes at the height of ten feet from the ground, and the tracks showed that the

animals had been feeding very quietly, and were probably not far distant. A few paces farther on, we came upon three great hollows in the
snow, their beds—whence they had risen not many minutes, as the
unfrozen surface showed.

"I most sure Capting," whispered Paul, pointing to a valley, grown
up with a dense shrubbery of young spruces and firs, "I most sure
moose lyin down agen in there. We go round and creep them. I most
'fraid though they smell us now."

The wind, unfortunately, was blowing lightly from us over the little valley. We had nearly finished the circuit to the opposite side of
the valley, and were preparing to enter the thick bush, when the

Indian exclaimed aloud, "Ah, dear, dear, I 'fraid bad luck—start um
moose, they get our wind when we were on other side."

On his pointing to where the snow had been brushed off the
leaves of laurustinus, which grew thickly between the evergreens, I
discovered their tracks, one foot point nearly overlapping the other,
and the distance between the tracks showed that the animals had
been started, going off at their usual pace, then when disturbed, a
long swinging trot. We made the best of our way back to the bundles,

and soon reached the shores of Fish Lake, where coming upon the track of our comrades, we followed them up to the opposite shore, and found all hands busily engaged in setting up the remains of an old camp, on a sloping bank, under some tall hemlocks. The camp poles, sheets of birch-bark, and other portions of the old tenement, had been found lying about in all directions, for it had not been visited for two years, and as fire-wood—of more importance even than shelter—had to be cut, our first night in it was rather uncomfortable. Luckily there was no wind. We two, who had been playing truant after the moose, were considerably rated. Two moose had been started from the immediate neighbourhood of the camp by my companion and the Indians on their arrival, and there was no doubt, from the numerous tracks and other signs, which had been seen on this side of the Gaspereau River, that the country was full of game. After sundown, the clouds, which had been discharging snow at intervals throughout the day, cleared off, and it began to freeze hard.

March 2: Awoke about an hour before daybreak, from the intense cold gripping my shoulder and side furthest from the fire, which, on shaking off my blanket, I found to be on its very last legs. My companion was awake too, and rustling about under his blanket in a most uneasy manner. Indians will sleep in any temperature, and require a large amount of rousing, so slipping on, with some trouble, my stiff frozen moccasins, I went out and returned with a few sticks, which, after blowing vigorously on the expiring members, were prevailed upon to ignite and emit a little warmth. Lighting our pipes, we squatted over the blaze, waiting for daylight and the awakening of the Indians. The forest trees were cracking in all directions from the intensity of the frost, some of them giving out a report like that of a pistol, and I heard the dismal hootings of the great horned owl, and the occasional bark of a fox, through the still frosty air, as distinctly as they had been uttered just outside the camp.

After breakfast, when guns were loaded, pipes lighted, and the usual lunch of a biscuit and a lump of cheese stowed away in our pockets, we started for the day's hunting. The morning was not well adapted for creeping, as there was no wind, without a small amount of which—enough to make music among the branches of the evergreens—it is very difficult to get within shooting distance of moose, in a thickly-wooded country.

The Fish Lake is a fine piece of water, four miles in length, from half-a-mile to a mile in breadth, and studded with numerous islands. Surrounded by fine hard-wood hills, the valleys between which were darkened by thick groves of evergreens, and with the firm ice to facilitate the walk from camp to any locality round its shores, the Fish Lake and its neighbouring forests appeared to hold out greater inducements to the moose-hunter, than any part of Nova Scotia I had yet seen.

After walking on the ice to the head of the lake, about two miles distant from our camp, we turned into the woods. Moose tracks, of various ages, were plentiful everywhere, but they were disregarded when we suddenly came upon fresh tracks of five caribou.

"Just gone by, Capting," said Williams, after a conversation in a low tone with old Paul. "Paul say, s'pose we no try moose this morning, as there's no wind—go after caribou."

"World Champion Bear Hunter" David Trueman Costley, Kings County, sporting the gold medal presented to him in 1897 by Queen Victoria. His story appears in Guides of the North Woods. *Born in 1838, Costley would have been one of the first white men to guide in Nova Scotia. In 1922, at the age of eighty-four, he killed his last bear—with a fence post!*

Of course we assented, it being always wrong to alter or dispute about any course of proceedings which your Indians may arrange, unless you are certain that they are not doing their best to show you sport. A few minutes' cautious walking through some thick greenwoods, which fringed the shore, brought us to one of the hard-wood hills, where, from the freshness of the tracks which now separated, it appeared that the caribou were feeding at no great distance. The acute eyes of our Indians detected spots on the bark of the maples, where the lichens had been recently pulled off.

We were all together—four of us—too many, when on the tracks of moose or caribou. There was no wind, and we expected, every instant, to see or hear signs of the game having started. Windfalls and dead wood lay about in every direction; and, now and then, a dead bough, buried in the snow, would snap under the moccasin, and cause everyone to turn round, with a look of despair at the offender. At length, the top of the hill was gained, and we were proceeding down the other side, when my companion stumbled against a rock concealed by the snow, and, endeavouring to save his fall by catching at an old yellow birch, which proved to be perfectly rotten—over it went with two or three sharp snaps—and fell down, with a dull crash, into the snow. A moment of anxious suspense ensued, the Indians straining their eyes and ears for some sign of the game, when I distinctly heard, in front, a sound of trotting in the snow, accompanied with sharp cracking of dead branches.

"Come along, gentlemen," said old Paul, setting off at full speed; and on we all went, helter-skelter, down the other side of the hill, getting many a roll over in the snow, and an occasional bruise in the

Sixth Lake Camp, Digby County, ca. 1890s. Major John Daley party. Major Daley is probably centre figure. Bear River Micmac guides to his left are,

standing L-R: Malti Pictou, John Lewis; seated on log shanty L-R: John McEwan, Louis Peters.

ankles, from kicking against frozen stumps, which projected everywhere.

On through some dark fir wood, at the foot of the hill, and we emerged on a large barren, just in time to see the caribou turn into the woods on the other side, four hundred yards distant. We now perceived that the Indians had given chase, knowing that they would cross the barren, and hoping to bring us out on it in time to get a shot.

"No use, Capting; I tink we sit down for spell, now, and have lunch. We have no luck to-day."

Brushing off the snow from a prostrate trunk, we sat down, and produced our biscuits and flasks.

"I suppose they won't stop for a long time, Paul," said I.

"Guess not—they gone to big bog on other side Tangier River, six mile away. They only hear us—no get our wind. S'pose they get our wind, they travel all day a'most."

Although you may walk through the woods of Nova Scotia for a whole day without seeing a sign of animal life, yet, on sitting down, hares, squirrels, moose-birds, and blue-jays will emerge from their hiding-places, and flit past you, either out of curiosity, or to scare you from their retreats. The blue-jays and squirrels, in particular, behaved in a most impertinent manner towards us, the former hopping on the branches of the trees overhead, and screaming loudly. The squirrels galloped about on the fallen trees, evidently in great wrath. Sometimes, raising themselves on their hind-legs, the hairs on their tail sticking out like those of a bottle-brush, they uttered their war-cry—a prolonged rattling scream. The hares, nearly white at this time of year, appear to be particularly stupid animals. We had great fun in pelting one—which, sitting in the snow a few yards off, took a most cool survey of our position—with snow-balls. Not an inch would he budge, till a well-directed ball from Williams caught him right on the nose, when he went off at a racing pace, clearing the windfalls in fine style.

On getting up, before we had advanced a hundred yards, the numerous tracks, freshly bitten boughs, and other signs, showed that a yard of moose was in the immediate neighbourhood, and the Indians, judging it best, from the want of necessary wind, to leave the animals undisturbed till a more favourable day should arrive, we made our way out cautiously to the ice, homewards bound. On the snow round the shores, there were innumerable tracks of loup-cerviers, called lucifees in this country, wild cats and otters, one of which latter animals I saw reposing on the surface of the lake, and prevented the formation of ice. I fired at but missed him, not having aimed low enough, for the otter dives at the flash like a coon.

The camp was a palace to what it had been when we started. Joe had woven round it, to the height of four feet from the ground, a thick covering of spruce boughs, and on entering, not a speck of daylight was to be seen through the sides. Internal improvements had taken place likewise. Sloping pillows of boughs, pinned onto reclining frames, had been erected for our heads, and birch bark baskets for tossing flasks and other pocket encumbrances into, on return to camp, constructed.

Joe said he had set some snares in the neighbourhood of the camp, for the hares that would be a great addition to our soup kettle, no fresh meat, fish, or fowl having been as yet brought in. In the evening, the sky became obscured from the south-west, and there were signs of its going to be "some sort of weather," as Paul said, next day.

March 3: The heavy, lead-coloured mass of cloud overhead this morning promised a fresh discharge of snow during the day. The old snow appeared to be rather softer, and, consequently, better for creeping, but there was no wind. Four fine hares, snared in Joe's wires last night, were brought into camp; their skins, &c., thrown outside soon attracted numbers of screaming moose-birds. This bird, called also the Canada jay, is always to be seen in the neighbourhood of a hunter's camp, into which they often have the audacity to venture, either through the door or smoke-hole, in search of their favourite food, flesh, as soon as it is vacated.

At breakfast, Joe affirmed that during the night he had heard a moose walk past the camp, and going a few yards up the hill, we found and followed the tracks to where he had been lying down till sunrise, when the chopping of fire-wood at the camp had startled him.

I left the camp in company with Williams, leaving my companion and old Paul to proceed in search of the moose yard, which had been discovered the day before. We turned into the woods at the bottom of the lake, and almost immediately found the fresh tracks of a yard of six moose. We followed them for an hour through country exceedingly difficult to creep in from the thick underwood, impenetrable groves of spruces, and swamps, the thin ice formed over which broke under our feet with a crack loud enough to start any moose that might be anywhere near.

We were still cautiously advancing on their tracks, when Williams suddenly rushed on up a hill, which was in front of us. I followed him, arriving at the top just in time to see a splendid bull moose, with a glossy coat, black as jet on the back and sides, bound over a windfall as he followed the rest of the yard, now out of sight. I fired at random and missed, of course, for I was completely out of breath, and the bull immediately disappeared behind the stems of a thick forest of hemlocks. Williams' acute ear had heard them start from the other side of the hill, and it seemed that the old bull we had seen was the leader of the yard, and had remained behind to ascertain the cause of alarm.

An hour afterwards we found the track of a single moose—a large bull—which we commenced creeping on. We had just crossed a swamp, the ice on which gave way with a crash at every step, and were standing talking in an undertone behind a mass of roots and earth formed by windfalls, when there was a tremendous crashing just on the other side. Williams, uttering an extraordinary bellow, in imitation of the call of a moose, stepped quickly aside, and discharged one barrel. I made a plunge through some thick spruces in hopes of catching a glimpse of the brute but without success. Williams' ball had not touched him as we found by there not being a trace of blood on the snow by the side of his tracks.

"Well, in all my life I never see moose act that way. Why, look here, Sir, where he lie down not five yards from where we stand talkin. I sure, too, we made noise enough comin 'cross that swamp to scare moose half mile off. We go home right off, I sick of our bad luck."

Though it certainly was provoking, it was some consolation to know that the country was full of moose, and that when a favourable day, with soft snow and plenty of wind should arrive, we might certainly expect some sport. Williams brought me out on the lake after a trudge of three miles in a course as straight as that of the crow, though he had never hunted through this country before. As we approached the camp, Williams, turning round, said with a grin of satisfaction: "Capting, other gentleman and old Paul home, and, I tink, shot moose; see little blood on the ice."

Outside the camp some fine steaks were hanging on a branch, and on squeezing through the little aperture which served as a door, we were greeted with cheers of success. My companion had killed a

The dinner was a feast to what our previous meals had been … and the frying-pan was in constant use for more than an hour.

moose, and had fired shots at two others without wounding them. The dinner was a feast to what our previous meals had been. Tender steaks, kidneys, marrow-bones, which were roasted in the ashes, and other delicacies, appeared as separate courses, and the frying-pan was in constant use for more than an hour. The Indians ate themselves perfectly torpid, Williams' particular morsel being the paunch, which he boiled and consumed to the last particle. My companion had

enjoyed his sport exceedingly, but had, unfortunately, sprained his ankle. Sleep overtook all of us earlier this evening than usual.

The fourth of March was a fine, calm morning. The hole in the ice through which water for the use of the camp was procured had been completely frozen up during the night, and had to be cut afresh. The lake was emitting a succession of booming sounds, which appeared to commence at one end, and to run with electric rapidity under the ice, to the other. These sounds, which are very grand on a large lake, show that the ice is gaining in thickness and strength. The woods, too, were giving evidence of the intensity of the frost by the loud cracking of their stems, resembling the undecided fire of a party of skirmishers, while the snow crunched under our moccasins with a noise ungrateful to the ear of a moose-hunter.

Paul had a slight attack of indigestion this morning, and set off into the woods in search of some Indian remedy. He put no faith in the cures which brandy is said to effect, in the old song, and refused, as Indians invariably will when in the bush, my proffered remedy–a cup of *bucketweech*–Anglice, brandy. His medicine proved to be the little purple berries of the ground juniper, which have a strong taste of turpentine, and which he bruised and swallowed in a cup of hot tea.

My companion's ankle was so stiff this morning, that he was obliged to remain in camp, so Paul and Williams both accompanied me when we started after breakfast. A fine breeze had now sprung up from the north-west, assisting us in our course down the lake, while the damp soles of our moccasins sticking to the surface of the glib ice, enabled us to run without danger of slipping. We turned into the woods, at nearly the same spot that Williams and myself had done the day before, and soon found the fresh track of an immense herd of moose. According to the Indian's computation, there could not have been less than sixteen or seventeen moose in the yard. At length, thought I, I shall get a shot at a moose. After a short consultation, in Micmac, between the Indians, in which the word *teeam* (moose), accompanied by gesticulations and pointings occurred frequently, the creeping commenced. Williams, carrying my rifle, took the lead; old Paul directing me to step in Williams' tracks, followed with his rusty musket.

The wind now blew steadily, and made melancholy music among the branches of the lofty hemlocks through which the chase led us, drowning the crackling of the

Guide Sam Soles, seventy-four, of Chezzetcook, Halifax County, another of the earliest white guides, ca. 1890s.

frozen snow under our moccasins. Still, our utmost caution was necessary, for the fine ear of the moose will, even in a gale of wind, detect the snapping of the smallest twig, or any noise foreign to the natural sounds of the forest, at a great distance.

Now is the time to see the Indian in his element and on his mettle. See how his eyes glisten as he bends down and scrutinizes the tall, slender stem of a young maple, the red, juicy top of which has been bitten off at the height of some nine or ten feet from the ground. Now he stoops and fingers the track, crumbling the lumps of snow dislodged by the huge foot, to tell the very minutes that have elapsed since the animal stood there.

On we go, every foot stepping in the track of the leading Indian, our

Let it be said that the bringing back of a trophy to adorn the smoking-room walls is not the only reward of a few weeks in the open after big game. The relief of a period of free, untrammeled life, for the time being independent of galling social fetters; the simple primitive pleasures of forest life in practically primeval hunting grounds; the constant lesson of that patient, persistent effort which Nature ever puts forth even in the rugged northern wilds, suggesting the ever-renewed struggle of humanity itself against opposing odds, altogether afford a pleasing experience which does not readily fade from the memory. Arthur Silver, 1907

arms employed in carefully drawing aside the branches which impede our progress, and preventing the barrels of our guns from noisy contact with the stems or boughs of the trees. The dense shrubbery of stunted evergreens, through which we had been worming our way for the last twenty minutes, appeared to be getting thinner, and we were about to emerge into an open space, with clumps of young hard-wood interspersed through a lofty grove of pines and hemlocks, when Williams suddenly withdrew his foot from a step which would have exposed him, and stepped behind a young spruce, his excited face beaming with delight as he beckoned me to advance.

There stood, or reposed, the stupendous animals in every variety of posture. Some were feeding, others standing lazily chewing the cud and flapping their broad ears, now and then stooping to snatch a mouthful of the pure snow. About fifty yards distant, in a clump of tall dead ferns and briars, stood a huge bull, with a splendid coat. Levelling at him, I discharged both barrels of my smooth bore, one at and the other behind the shoulder. He dropped, and the rest of the yard, discovering their foes, plunged off through the bushes, knocking over the dead trees in their way as if they had been nine-pins.

Williams, thrusting my rifle into my hands, pointed to a fine cow, which was the hindmost of the retreating yard. I fired both barrels at her, as she showed herself in an open space between the trees, at about eighty yards distance. A slight stumble and an increased acceleration in her speed told us that she was hit.

"I think we shall get the cow, Paul," said I loading away. No sooner were the words out of my mouth, than the bull, which we thought to have been *hors-de-combat,* scrambling up, dashed off gloriously after the retreating yard on three legs.

"Come along with me, Sir," shouted Paul. "Williams, you take gentleman's rifle, and go kill cow."

We dashed on at full speed after the bull, who was nearly out of sight, and was shaping his course as a wounded moose always does, through the thickest covers of the bush. However, the poor brute left traces of his direction, which gave him little chance of eluding our pursuit, for the blood on the snow lay in a line nearly a foot in breadth. A few minutes brought us to where he had been standing to rest and listen, as a circular pool of blood on the snow indicated, and we presently caught a glimpse of him going gallantly up a steep hill, about a hundred yards in advance. Several times I dropped on one knee and levelled, but the stems of the hemlocks were so broad and frequent, and my hand so unsteady, that before I could bring the barrels to bear on him, he was again out of sight.

On arriving at the top of the hill, I was completely used up, as we had followed him at great speed for nearly half a mile. I had lost my cap, and powder flask, bullets, and biscuits jolted out of my pockets, in the frequent rolls-over which I had received, were lying in the snow at intervals between us and the spot where the chase commenced. However, we must persevere, for the blood had nearly ceased, and if he escaped in his present wounded condition, he would die.

Blacks guided as well, although not in great numbers. Many of those who did worked the New France area behind Weymouth, which was popular with sportsmen in the early 1900s. Pictured here is guide Ed Barr, eighty-six, at Riverdale, Digby County.

As luck would have it, on entering a little barren, we saw the moose standing at the other end, evincing no signs of wishing to make a fresh start. Shaking the snow out of the barrels and putting on fresh caps, I dropped him with one ball, and immediately advancing, I fired the second barrel at his head, aiming behind the ear. Down went his head into the snow, and with a convulsive quiver he stretched out dead.

"Well done, skipper," said old Paul, slapping me on the back. "You done well to-day. A most splendid bull," continued he, lifting up the huge head of the moose off the snow.

I own that I felt completely triumphant. Perhaps the hard chase we had gone through before killing him, and my many previous disappointments in getting shots at moose had made me callous, but not the least remorse did I feel at having extinguished life in so huge an animal. Besides, it was my first moose. He measured nearly seven feet from the hoof to the shoulder, and we calculated that he must have weighed eleven or twelve hundred pounds. And the spot, too, was so wildly picturesque. It was a small circular area in the forest, and the bright scarlet leaves of the ground laurels peeped through the snow. He had fallen under a black spruce, which appeared to spread its massive snow-laden branches over him as the funereal cypress.

Seated on a log opposite, and lighting my pipe, I watched with great satisfaction the butchering process, which Paul performed with the evident ease and skill of an old hand. The moose-birds soon made their appearance, and hopped round boldly, almost within reach. Ravens and crows wheeled in circles overhead, croaking horribly, waiting for our departure, to commence their feast on the offal. Paul finished by shovelling snow into the interior of the carcass, which was, by our united efforts, placed on its belly and thatched over with spruce boughs and a thick coating of snow. In this state, the carcass of a moose will keep, provided the wolves and lynxes do not get wind of it, till the breaking up of the winter.

In the meantime, we had heard two sharp cracks from my rifle, with which Williams had gone after the wounded cow moose; so Paul, binding on to his belt a goodly bunch of steaks and other delicate morsels for home consumption, started in search of him. Near the spot whence we imagined we had heard the sound of the rifle to have proceeded, the old Indian uttered the dismal cry of the horned owl. An answer was at once returned from a spot not far distant, and on going up, we found Williams, with bared arms, busily engaged over the carcass of the cow moose. He had shot her after a race similar to ours.

Great were the rejoicings in camp that evening, after our late arrival. My companion had been down to the river, and with a long stick as a rod, two or three yards of twine, and a hook, baited first with salt pork, and afterwards with pieces of their own flesh, had caught several dozen fine trout, averaging a pound in weight a-piece, and which proved to be remarkably fine and well-flavoured, considering the time of year.

March 5: After lying awake for some time this morning listening to

John Bradley was a well-known black hunting and fishing guide from Wellington, Grand Lake. He was born at Annapolis Royal, on March 18, 1836, and died at Wellington September 3, 1930, at ninety-four years of age. This photo was taken in 1926. He acted as guide for the Duke of York (later King George) when he visited Nova Scotia around 1902.

the owls and foxes, I got up, and squatting over the fire, lighted my pipe. I like thinking over the episodes of a day's moose-hunting, recalling the scenery passed over, and the little incidents which had enlivened the trudge through the woods: the excitement of the sport, the display of sagacity on the part of your Indian hunter, whose motions you watch as you would those of a well-trained hound, and the wholesome feeling of freedom which accompanies you at all times in the bush strike the imagination more forcibly on after reflection.

After breakfast, my comrade's ankle being nearly well from numerous applications of brandy, used as a lotion, we all proceeded together down the lake. At the lowest extremity of the Fish Lake, a narrow belt of ground, covered with dense greenwoods, separated it from a chain of smaller lakes. We were walking on the bank of a little rocky brook, which trickled through this isthmus, when old Paul stopped and said, "I got notion of something, Capting. I most sure moose in hard-wood hill, away down shore of the smaller lake. S'pose one go along with me and Williams, to creep, and other gentleman stop here. S'pose we start moose—he very likely run through, just here, and then, whoever stop, have grand chance."

It certainly was likely that a moose, if started from the woods on the north shore, would endeavour to gain the cover of the dense greenwood forests on the south side of the lake, which, as these animals rarely venture on the ice, could only be accomplished by passing through this belt of woods. It was about three hundred yards in breadth, and, from its centre, the ice on both lakes could be seen through the trees, so that any large animal, like a moose, running through it, must pass within range of the gun of a sportsman concealed half-way between the lakes.

I volunteered to remain here, on the chance, while my companion proceeded, in company with the two Indians, to hunt through the fine hard-wood hills on the north shore of the lakes. As they would have to proceed nearly three miles before turning into the woods to hunt, I determined to make myself comfortable over a fire, and by the help of my pipe, for the next hour at least. Near the centre of this isthmus were the remains of an old bear trap. Cutting a lot of spruce boughs, I placed them on the ground in the old dead fall, which, having kindled a merry little blaze outside, I entered and lighted my pipe, my guns, both ready for immediate service, leaning against the trunk of an adjacent hemlock. At first, I thought I should not be able to hear the sound of approaching steps, from the confusing gurgling sounds produced by the water in the little brook trickling under the ice.

However, my ears soon became accustomed to it, and to the murmuring of the wind through the lofty foliage of the hemlocks.

As far as I could see into the forest, on the side whence I expected the moose to make their appearance, the ground sloped gently down towards the brook which ran in front of my position. Thick masses of stunted firs rose up everywhere between the lofty forest trees, to the height of some ten or twelve feet. My pipe going out, I fell into a reverie, which turned to drowsiness, and, at length, notwithstanding several startlings which I received from the sudden chattering of a squirrel, or the tapping of a woodpecker on a dead trunk, to a sound sleep.

I don't know what woke me again, whether it was from the cold, or any unusual noise, for I awoke with a start, and with the full expectation of finding a huge moose standing over me, and threatening retribution for the death of his comrades on the day previous. My little fire had burnt itself out, evidently some time ago, and my feet were completely benumbed. I had scarcely risen when I heard something like a tread in the snow, though whence the sound proceeded, I could not at first tell. Hearing it again, accompanied by a slight crack of a bough, I made up my mind that something was walking in the snow, on the opposite side of the run. It might be my companion and the Indians returning; if not, it surely must be a moose.

There was a large pine near me, over-hanging the brook, and, crouching behind it with my two guns, I waited in breathless expectation. The tramping soon came nearer, and, by its stopping at intervals, I knew that it must proceed from moose, travelling cautiously. At length, I saw the top of one of the dwarf spruces shake, and heard two or three sharp snaps of dead wood. A minute afterwards, two gigantic heads protruded from the evergreens, looking cautiously around and sniffing the air rather suspiciously. I was more than once afraid that they would get my wind, as the currents of air are very undecided in a valley; however, to my great relief, I saw their ears resume a hanging position, and the bushes again wave, as they forced their way onward.

After two minutes of dreadful suspense, the leader, a huge cow moose, stood on the opposite bank, about ten yards in front of my tree. She was just descending into the brook, and, in another instant, would have brushed past the pine so closely, that I should have been able to pull the bristles from her coat, when I levelled at her enormous head and fired. She fell dead in her tracks. The bull, as moose always will at the report of a gun, appeared stupefied for an instant, but seeing me stoop to pick up my undischarged rifle, threw back his head, and went off briskly along the opposite bank.

Rushing along the bank, in a course parallel to his, I at length got a view of him through an opening in the trees, and fired both barrels simultaneously. As I hastily reloaded, I could still hear him crashing along through the dead wood. The cow was quite dead. Not knowing whether the bull was wounded or not, I crossed the brook and followed up his tracks to where he had been at the time of my shot. Here were a few drops of blood, and proceeding half-a-dozen yards farther, a broad trail of blood on the snow shewed that he was hit hard on the left side. Pushing along through dense thickets, with my arm up to protect my face, a sudden sound caused me to look up, when I found that I had stumbled suddenly on my moose, who made a desperate attempt at rising, but failed. A ball behind the ear finished him. When I gave vent to my triumphant feelings in a loud yell, to my surprise, it was answered by another, at no great distance, and, in a few minutes, Williams emerged from the bushes, and stood looking with a grin of satisfaction, first at me, and then at the moose, simply remarking, "You done well."

He said that my companion and Paul, having heard my shots at a great way off, had despatched him to my assistance. They had started, without having obtained a shot at the two moose that, unluckily for themselves, had attempted to cross the isthmus from a hard-wood hill, about two miles distant, and were now hunting round to the north of the big lake.

After performing the usual operation on the carcasses with his hunting knife, he bound onto his belt the choice morsels, and accompanied me back to camp. At dusk, my companion and Paul arrived, fatigued though also triumphant. Soon after Williams had left them, they had wounded a moose, one of an immense yard of ten, and after a chase of nearly four miles, through most difficult country, had shot the animal in the act of crossing a jam of ice on the Tangier

River, a distance of at least eight miles from camp. This was our best day, and great feasting and merriment went on in camp till long after the usual hour of stretching out.

We had now six moose lying in the woods at various distances from camp, and it was proposed by old Paul, and unanimously agreed to by the whole party, that hunting should cease, and that the more laborious operation of hauling out the meat from the woods to the lake should commence on the morrow.

Micmac hunting camp near Weymouth ca. 1900. The sled, right, would have been similar to those carved by Hardy's guides.

March 6: The Indians, early this morning, commenced making a hand-sled on which to drag the moose-meat over the ice. Chopping out the different pieces roughly, they brought them into camp, and taking out their whittling knives, were soon nearly buried in shavings.

The knife, which the Indian uses in manufacturing anything out of wood, is a beautifully-tempered thin blade, curving backwards at the point. The handle is curved also, and there is a semicircular indentation at the end, for the ball of the thumb to rest in. In cutting and paring, the Indian, pressing the piece of wood firmly against his chest with the left hand, holds his knife in his right, back downwards, and cuts towards him. They appear to possess immense power in detaching thick splinters by this mode of using the knife, while they can pare off long shavings as finely as if a plane had been used.

The hand-sled, when finished, turned out to be a platform, about two feet broad and four long, resting upon runners, cut out of rock maple, turned up in front, and beautifully smoothed so as to run well over the ice.

A horse and crude sled are used to haul out moose and gear near Liscomb Mills, Guysborough County, ca. 1921.

After breakfast, they started to the spot where lay the farthest of the carcasses, and my companion accompanied me down the river about a quarter of a mile past its exit from the lake, with the intention of trouting. Here there was a spot, where, from the velocity of the current, the ice had not formed, and in which trout may always be taken with bait on a fine day during the winter months. The rods were there, and we had brought lines and hooks; but where was the bait? We had forgotten to bring a lump of salt pork. One is not long, however, in finding expedients in this country, so, cutting off a bit of my untanned moccasin, I baited with it, and made a cast among the rapids. Before it had fairly disappeared beneath the surface, it was taken with shark-like ferocity. The rod was a strong one, and there being no fear of the line going, out he came, over my head, and fell with a plump on the snow behind, where he was seized by my companion, who speedily converted the whitest portion of him into bait. I believe that the trout would have risen at a scarlet hackle, for they seemed to refuse nothing, and were wonderfully lively for the time of year. As many trout as we could conveniently carry were caught in the course of an hour, and we returned to camp, where some of them were fried for lunch. The remainder of the day was spent in shooting partridges round the camp, practising with the axe, snaring moose-birds, and similar amusements.

The Indians returned late, rather fagged, having brought the carcasses of two moose out to the edge of the lake. Joe broke his pipe short off this evening, and I was much amused by his plan of making a wooden stem, in which to insert the bowl. Cutting a cylindrical piece of soft wood, about a foot in length and an inch in diameter, he notched it at one end, so that it appeared like a child's pop-gun, with the ramrod slightly projecting. After allowing it to remain for a few minutes in the hot ashes, he took it in his hands, and holding the projecting knob firmly between his teeth, twisted it round several times, and finally drew out a mass of fibres attached to the knob. After finishing up neatly with a few fantastic devices, the wooden tube, he inserted the remaining stem of his pipe into it. The smoke draws deliciously cool through one of these long wooden stems, and I prevailed on him to exert his ingenuity in making me several.

March 7: The frost this morning was intense; it must have been at least ten or twelve degrees below zero. However, there was no wind to circulate the frozen particles of air, and we were all comfortable enough inside the camp. All hands left the camp after breakfast this morning, to haul out the moose, proceeding first to the spot where my first bull had fallen. We found the carcass intact, though all the offal had been consumed by ravens and moose-birds.

The hide was first taken off, and then after a few chops with the axe, and a dexterous cut or two with the hunting-knife, the huge mass lay in four quarters, weighing nearly two hundred weight a-piece. The Indians, each taking one of them on the back, holding on in front by the leg, which bent downwards over their shoulders, marched off with apparent ease, while we, slinging a quarter on a pole resting on our shoulders, followed them, every now and then beseeching them to stop to rest. The remaining moose was served in the same way, and we returned to camp long after dusk, feeling that we had done the hardest day's work yet.

The Indians appeared excessively amused when we tried to repeat casual Micmac words, the meaning of which we had learnt. For instance, instead of asking Joe for "more tea," we would say *"Eganamooi abstch potacwae,"* at which they would go off into fits of laughter, and puff away furiously at their pipes saying, "You get along well, Capting, speak all same as one Ingin."

This was our last night in camp, as we wished to be in Halifax in two days time.

March 8: After breakfast we made arrangements for the removal of the whole moose-meat, excepting one carcass, which we gave to old Paul, to

It is a misconception that moose hunting was a popular sport in Nova Scotia for non-residents. On average only 100-150 licenses were sold annually. Moose were pursued mainly by British officers and residents. Most non-resident sports in the early 1900s came for the tranquility offered by fishing and camping during the warmer months. This trend changed following World War II when deer hunting became the primary attraction.

Halifax. This would be attended with some labour and difficulty, for a road would have to be made, by felling and clearing the forest for eight miles through the woods, over which the meat was to be dragged by a team of oxen on a sled. Having settled that Williams was to go in to the settlement to engage two men and a team of oxen, and that all hands should remain in camp till it was all properly finished, we started under the guidance of Joe for a walk of eight miles through the woods, in a driving snow-storm, which made it anything but agreeable. Four hours saw us once more under a roof, before a table covered with broiled ham, fresh eggs, butter and milk, luxuries to which we had been strangers for some time, and what was most acceptable of all, some thoroughly good London porter.

We sleighed in to Halifax by the afternoon of the following day, and in the course of a week had the satisfaction of seeing the arrival of the whole of our trophies, drawn by a team of four horses. The meat was proved to be in excellent order, and was universally approved of, by the numerous friends and others amongst whom it was distributed.

Thus ended successfully and very satisfactorily, our ten days hunting in the woods down East.

CHAPTER 5

GEORGE N. TRICOCHE
British writer,
early 1900s

CAPE BRETON CARIBOU

It happened this way. We met perchance in the dining-room of a Liverpool hotel. The six of us had been sitting three times a day, for a week, at the same table; but, with the exception of two ladies apparently related to each other, and who exchanged occasional and uninteresting remarks, we were utter strangers to one another; and, not having been introduced, remained silent, until, one evening, out of a clear sky came down the spark that was to kindle our friendship. The elder of the two ladies, whom I had mentally labelled "The Spinster," confided to the younger one, rather tremulously, that she had forgotten to inquire about the sailing time, on the next day, of the steamer *Regina*. It was too late to telephone to the booking office. What could she do? Oh dear! These boats have a way of starting at such impossible hours: perhaps this particular one departs at sunrise, who knows? Her companion did not reply, but looked somewhat dismayed. It was pathetic—but not for long. The steamship's name, *Regina,* was evidently familiar to the four men at the table, for a sudden interest appeared simultaneously on their features; they raised their eyes from their respective plates, and each one seemed about to say something. Circumstances warranted a breach of the traditional English

Postcard depicting the wilds of Nova Scotia ca. 1907.

In the wilds of Nova Scotia

reserve among unpresented persons.

"Pardon me, madam," said a man with a military bearing, "do you mean the boat of the White Star Dominion Line, bound for Halifax and Portland?"

"Yes, sir."

"I happen to leave by this steamer to-morrow, and may give you the information you want; she sails at 2 p.m."

"I am booked on the *Regina,* too!" exclaimed impulsively his right-hand neighbour, who had a strong French accent.

"As a matter of fact, I am bound for Halifax on the same craft," remarked a dignified-looking individual.

"So am I!" added the writer.

And the ice was broken!

It turned up later that we were all, more or less, "on pleasure bent," and that our respective objects were not so absorbing or exclusive as to preclude travelling together, at least for several weeks. The idea was The Girl's, nobody else's; but it suited us perfectly, for each one, at the bottom of his heart, was deploring to go alone on his way.

The gentleman with the martial demeanour was an army captain, taking advantage of a short leave of absence to go hunting caribous in Nova Scotia; he thought it "great fun" to have us all, and especially the ladies, accompany him through the wilds of Cape Breton. The youth with Gallic features, a recent *agrégé* of the Paris University, whose hobby appeared to be the history of New France, intended to visit what territories were once Acadia, and study their population, before reporting for duty at a *Lycée* in Brittany; he was only too pleased to find fellow travellers able to understand his English, and willing to try their French on him. As for the dignified personage, his visiting card introduced him as a F.R.S.S. and F.S.A.E.—whatever that may be; he had no definite plans, save to rest after a period of over-work; and was going to Halifax as he might have gone to Bermuda or Madeira. Yet, as he belonged to Edinburgh, he would turn his trip to good account by studying the Scotch of Nova Scotia. At all events, The Scholar was polite enough to inform us that to travel in our midst would be a pleasant diversion; but a diversion from what—this remained in the dark.

It goes without saying that we made no effort to ascertain the motives that prompted the two ladies to choose Nova Scotia for a vacation land at a time of the year when most people who have been summering there go back home. Perhaps they wanted to act differently from other tourists. Again, it may be that, womanlike, they had no more reason to do this than to do anything else.

As regards the writer, since his work required much travelling through the Maritime Provinces, he thought that there was nothing to lose, and probably much to gain by joining a party of cultured,

The elderly lady, who had never been on a camping trip before, would have carried along enough victuals to start a summer hotel—Edith, on the contrary … wished to put us on half rations, and to try upon our respective constitutions a variety of so-called "Sportsman's Foods"—a fearful array of dried up, dehydrated, evaporated atrocities.

congenial persons whose observations and points of view might be valuable to him.

To organize a party is one thing, to get it started is another, and harder proposition, especially when it numbers among its members representatives of the fair sex. In this particular case, The Spinster and The Girl caused us some delay, and still more annoyance by their radically divergent views concerning dress, saddles, baggage, food, and about everything connected with the trip. The elder woman, of course, had ultra-conservative ideas on all these subjects, while the younger female flatly refused to observe what her aunt called "conventions and proprieties," and, notably, to wear a riding habit, and to use a side-saddle.

"Is this Rotten Row or the wilderness?" she asked The Spinster indignantly. She wanted a pair of breeches, a khaki shirt, and a "cow puncher" hat. Finally, at the eleventh hour, to our intense relief, they compromised on a "divided skirt." The saddle question adjusted itself, for there was only one kind to be had—"the man's kind being good enough for both sexes," so said our host. Besides, the latter had never seen the "side one," and did not know that "such contraptions existed." But the worst was still to come. When the problem of food arose, the breach between The Girl and The Spinster widened. The elderly lady, who had never been on a camping trip before, would have carried along enough victuals to start a summer hotel of the fashionable kind. Edith, on the contrary, who had, unfortunately for us, studied Domestic Science, and obtained somewhere a diploma of Dietitian, wished to put us on half rations, and to try upon our respective constitutions a variety of so-called "Sportsman's Foods"—a fearful array of dried up, dehydrated, evaporated atrocities. The guide whom we had engaged was bewildered when he saw the list carefully concocted by The Girl.

"Give me the regular camp fare; bacon and coffee, some condensed milk, and I'll do the rest. We shall kill enough fowl or fish enough trouts on the way not to bother with carrying all this fancy stuff!"

This outburst almost infuriated both women; and, for a while, things looked dark. At the bottom of our hearts, The Scholar, The Parisian and myself began to wish The Spinster and her lively niece would give up the trip. But The Captain, who was recognized leader of the expedition, declared with finality that the guide alone would be in charge of the commissariat. And thus peace was restored!

One point upon which we all agreed was the necessity for warm clothing. True, it was not yet autumn, but, in this part of Canada, nights are really cold in September—and some days almost so, when the sun is not shining. Fortunately, at Sydney, before leaving for Ingonish, we had provided ourselves with dark woollen coat-sweaters, woollen caps fitting fairly tight, and the traditional footwear of the Canadian woodsman: the *shoepack*. This is a kind of moccasin, oil tanned and waterproof, in which the edges of the soles are turned up and sewn to the upper. It is lucky that we should have met our guide at Sydney, our base of supplies, because he gave us very good advice. For instance, he prevented the Parisian from buying a brown sweater, on account, of the danger of being mistaken, in the woods, for a deer, by other huntsmen. He explained to us that conditions differed from those in New Brunswick.

Women may share the joys of camping here with perfect comfort, there is practically no hard work to be done, and the beds are warm and good. The nights are often very cold, even in June and July, and warm underclothing should be taken, with thin stuff for the middle of the day, should it be required.

Eddie Breck

"Over there," he said, "accidents among non-resident sportsmen are practically unknown, because guides have exclusive territories about 25 miles by 15; therefore, the possibility of a sportsman being shot by mistake is very remote. In Cape Breton, such is not the case; a hunting or fishing party may come across another one at any time."

We were to cover, on horseback, the twenty or twenty-five miles separating us from the Caribou Country, which lies towards the Cheticamp River. This could have been done easily in one day, had there been any road worthy of the name. But we had only a trail at our disposition; and, several of us being of the "tenderfoot" species, it was decided to take two days for the trip.

We were eight, including the guide and his assistant, a young fellow who was to act as "boy of all works." Each of us, except the boy, had a saddle horse, upon which was strapped a duffle bag, containing all his or her belongings. Supplies and cooking utensils were carried by two pack animals of a nondescript variety; our demand for saddle horses had exhausted the ordinary equine resources of Ingonish and vicinity, and it has never been made clear to us where the sad pack specimens had been exhumed from. Their hirsute, shaggy appearance was wretched enough; yet, nothing compared with their disconsolate, bewildered eyes that seemed to reproach us for every ounce of burden imposed upon the sorry backs of the creatures. The Spinster assured us that she could not look at them in the face without feeling like bursting into profuse apologies, and that she would fain have preferred to carry the packs herself. But, oh, how illogically a woman's brain works, sometimes! The next minute, said Spinster, stopping her horse suddenly, was asking with alarm "where the trunks were." And, as this caused some merriment, she looked at us in consternation: "Did you ever think I would go travelling with these … er … duffle bags?" The Captain, very gravely, assured the good lady that it had never occurred to us that she could be guilty of such a *faux pas:* but circumstances over which we had no control compelled us all to take a step back towards the uncivilized state. As she was apparently wondering whether the officer had made fun of her or not, a diversion was caused by a discussion between The Captain and the guide about the best calibre of rifle for moose- or caribou-hunting. The former thought that the ideal gun was the English Express Rifle, a bullet from which, should it strike a moose anywhere between the tail and the ears, will bring him to the ground. But the guide asserted, with reason, that experience had shown this to be a rather extreme view of the case. A modern high-power rifle of not less than thirty calibre, and using a soft-nosed bullet, will, if aimed straight, do the trick. There is this disadvantage, however, in using a rifle of small calibre, that a wounded moose or caribou leaves behind a very indistinct blood trail, which has a tendency to improve his chances of making a get-away.

The first stage of our little journey was somewhat trying to the three "tenderfoot" of the expedition, namely The Spinster, The Scholar, and The Parisian. The road was rather rough and rocky, the sun hot, and the breeze very chilly. When we reached the camping ground, a barren-looking spot by the side of a stream, the elderly lady cast dismal glances in all directions, with the vague hope of discovering, if not a country inn, at least some barn.

"I thought," she said, "that 'camp,' in this part of Canada, meant some kind of rustic bungalow or lodge, such as I have seen described on all the folders, guide books and advertising matter."

The guide explained to her that these luxuries did exist, but only on the ordinary hunting or fishing "territories." "Wherever there is a regular flow of sportsmen, guides have arranged to give the latter the maximum possible of comfort."

A typical Nova Scotia guide's camp.

"This is precisely what I dislike in your North American hunting," interrupted The Captain. "I do not exactly blame you," laughed the guide; "yet most sportsmen that come from the 'States' to the Maritimes are not of the truculent kind. Many are just lawyers, brokers, sedentary fellows, you know, who scarcely take any exercise all year round, save during their vacation. They think they are sportsmen; in reality, they do not enjoy 'roughing it.' "

"I see," remarked The Parisian, "regular Tartarians!"

The guide looked at him dubiously, and went on: "Anyway, the guides, in the region of the Maritimes where game is plentiful, have found out by experience that their patrons like to have things made as comfortable and snug as possible. Log cabins are built at convenient places, provided with stoves, good chairs, bunks, etc. While a bed of fir boughs is all right to talk about, it is not the most agreeable thing in the world to sleep upon; therefore several guides, especially in New Brunswick, have introduced the spring bed in their camps."

"Gracious! Why not bath-rooms, when they were bent on taking all the picturesque out of the life in the open?" grumbled The Captain.

"Well, sir," replied the guide, "these, and even telephone booths are found in some up-to-date Maine camps. Of course, here, in Cape Breton, there are no ready-made camps. That would not pay, for caribou hunting is not frequent; and, besides, this kind of game is protected, at times, for a long period of years. So, we shall have to camp in the rough old style."

"For which I am most thankful!" concluded the officer with emphasis.

Notwithstanding the guide's premonition, we spent a pleasant evening and night at our camp with good blankets, the fir boughs proved better than our untrained members expected; and the guide had been thoughtful enough to supply the two ladies with sleeping

We spent a pleasant evening and night at our camp with good blankets, the fir boughs proved better than our untrained members expected.

bags. However, what I enjoyed above all was the conversation around the camp-fire. The guide was a picturesque speaker, who had either observed a great deal, or read considerably about the men in his profession, and Canadian "backwoods men" in general.

The Girl could restrain herself no longer. "Will someone please tell me something about Indians?" she almost shrieked.

The guide laughed: "I am afraid all the blood-curdling tales about the Indians are pretty stale by this time. Yet, for lack of anything else and better, I may tell you a fact that shows how clever observers our Micmacs are. Once, in a wooded region, we were looking for a certain settlement of white men. After walking several hours in the forest, we came upon a trail which, without doubt, had been travelled lately by a wagon. This was a relief for us; yet, in which direction should we proceed to reach the settlement? We were much embarrassed; the road was going north-south; we went northwards at random. But the Indian of our party saw pretty soon a wisp of hay that had dropped close to a tree on the trail. 'Well,' said the Micmac, 'we might find a good clue. When a tree knocks off a handful of hay from a cart, that hay falls *on the side of the tree to which the cart is going.*

The Spinster enjoyed travelling out of the beaten paths. She had heard much about the "wilds" of north-eastern Nova Scotia, and was looking forward with pride to the time when, in the cosy home of Bayswater, she would relate her thrilling experiences to a cenacle of sedentary friends.

Now, let me see: the hay lies *on our side* of the trunk, so we going on the direction from which the wagon came.' We were delighted at this discovery. But our leader, an old hand, put a damper to our glee. 'That's all right,' he said, 'but how do you know that by going to the direction from which the hay came we shall reach the settlement? Could not that be, most likely, hay brought in from natural meadows to the settlers' cabins? In that case, we should go the other way to find the settlement.'... 'No mistake,' replied the Indian grinning. 'This hay is *salted;* therefore it comes *from* the meadows near the settlement, since the farmers salt their hay to keep it. The load was probably sent out by the settlers to some camp, in order to feed teams of oxen used in hauling timber.' Such was indeed the case, for three miles farther we arrived at the houses!"

"To-night, we shall reach the Indian village," casually remarked the guide, next morning at breakfast.

The Girl started so petulantly that she nearly upset the camp table. "At last," she cried, "I shall see some real Indians!"

"Do be careful, dear," said her aunt, "you will break all our cups and saucers!"

"Bah!" replied the irrepressible Edith, "they are all tin things; one could not smash them if one tried. You always forget that we are camping, aunty dear!"

"I do not see why you are so anxious to meet these Indian men," retorted The Spinster. "What kind are they, anyway?" she added, addressing The Captain.

"Micmacs," said the officer, "that is all I know about them."

This was our last stage towards the Caribou Country, and we were anxious to reach our goal as speedily as possible. The Captain, undoubtedly in a hurry to shoot his caribou, was asking the guide, now and then, questions about the haunts and habits of this new kind of a game—which, however, he was somewhat inclined to despise as hardly worthy of the attention of a veteran of tiger hunts in Bengal. The rest of the party did not care very much for the real object of the expedition; each one had his or her own whim. The Spinster enjoyed travelling out of the beaten paths. She had heard much about the "wilds" of north-eastern Nova Scotia, and was looking forward with pride to the time when, in the cosy home of Bayswater, she would relate her thrilling experiences to a cenacle of sedentary friends. To The Parisian, every square mile of Cape Breton was sacred land, fraught with recollections of a glorious and romantic past; the more rugged the country became, the better his imagination could depict to him the struggles and the hardships of the early French pioneers that followed in the tracks of Cartier. It would be difficult to find out what the thoughts of The Scholar were; most likely he simply kept in readiness to shower with dates and statistics anyone who, within his hearing, would venture to ask a question. So The Girl and the writer, who were riding, one in front of him, the other right behind, kept their impressions for themselves. But Edith confessed later that this was the hardest part of the trip.

When, towards noon, we reach the end of our journey through the woods, we are surprised at the aspect of what the guide had pompously described as "The Indian Village." It consists of two shacks and half a dozen tents, apparently bought at some second-hand store dealing in discarded army goods. True, there is some cooking done on a camp-fire; and the smell that rises from it is far from engaging. But the dusky woman who watches it is seated in a regular camp chair, very modern, and reading an old number of the ubiquitous Canadian magazine, *MacLean,* at the fashion page. One or two old Micmac women are weaving baskets or embroidering moccasins; but a younger one, not unattractive, and her hair bobbed in the latest style, is sewing a kimono with the help of a MacCall pat-

Micmac camp—tent and spruce-bark wigwam ca. 1915.

tern! This is a little too much for The Captain, who turns to the guide and says contemptuously: "Do you call this an Indian encampment?"

"Well," replies the guide, somewhat ruffled, "what did you expect to find here? Cannibals feasting on 'missionary pie'?"

"Sir," interrupts The Spinster, "such language ..."

"At any rate," says the officer, "I should not be astonished! I told you before that I did not believe in Canada Indians. By Jove, give me equatorial Africa for local colour. It is bad enough to behold a railroad on the banks of Lake Victoria Nianza; but at least, one finds some real natives there!"

The guide explained that these Micmacs come to this place only for the hunting and fishing season.

"Worse still," grumbled The Captain, "they are mere Micmac tourists!"

Yet, in spite of The Captain's assertion, we saw some interesting things at that camp. Eels are fished, sometimes, in a peculiar manner; but we were too early at Cape Breton to watch the proceeding, for it is used mostly at the full moon of October—so they told us. It seems the Micmacs place in the water a rather long basket, large at one end and much narrower at the other, which connects with a wooden sluice leading up to the surface. The eels, apparently, enjoy the sport of going up the incline—a reverse kind of "shooting the chutes!"—and are easily caught by the fisherman waiting in a canoe. On some spots, these fishes are extremely numerous; fishing, then, is done by all the members of the family together, and we were assured that, at times, a single household can get thirty canoe loads of eels in a day. One may wonder what they are doing with it! An old woman told us that the eels are dumped into a hole at the bottom of which are very hot ashes. There, they disgorge their slime, after which they may be smoked like any other fish. To the Micmacs, as well as to the Abenakis of Maine, eels appear to be a very dainty morsel. They are careful to keep an ample supply of them in store for the winter months.

The Girl who, in spite of her aunt's vehement protests, was mingling freely with the Indian women, announced triumphantly to us that she had learnt how to smoke eels, in the most approved Micmac fashion. A wide but rather shallow hole is dug in the ground and filled with very hot embers from birch wood. A number of forked sticks are driven in the soil all around the hole, and support other sticks placed, thus, horizontally above the fire. All these sticks, of course, are of green wood, not liable to catch fire easily. The fishes are disposed upon that kind of wattling. New embers are added constantly, and the eels smoked day and night for a week or more. The

Girl thought this was very useful to know. As The Spinster observed sarcastically that she doubted it, inasmuch as said Girl's home was in Bayswater, too respectable and conservative a suburb for a performance of the kind.

"Why," The Girl replied serenely, "we can do it at our country home in the Devonshire!"

"Never!" exclaimed the indignant aunt, "not as long as I live shall we do such primitive cooking on my beautiful estate!"

Cape Breton Micmac guide 'Gabriel' ca. 1900.

"At any rate," said the accommodating Girl, "there is something I can try right here. I shall bake bread *à la* Micmac. You just get flat stones, heat them, and pour the dough on them without using any dish."

Whether the experiment was made or not I never knew. But one evening, our young friend placed on our table an excellent ruffed grouse—commonly known in Nova Scotia as birch partridge—that had been cooked according to the Indian culinary rules. That is to say, wrapped up, without being plucked, in a thick coat of reddish clay, and placed on a moderate fire. On due time, the mould is broken, and falls off with the feathers. The dish is very savoury, probably because nothing had been lost of the natural juice of the meat.

The Captain (who was, in fact, the only Nimrod of the party), although a great respecter of game laws, could not help complaining that the caribou season should not coincide with that of many other animals, such as hare, mink, otter, fox or raccoon. We were too early for these; and the time of the officer was limited. Besides, pheasant, spruce partridge, and deer are absolutely protected in Cape Breton. The Captain was anxious to kill a moose, as the latter and the caribou were the only game at which he never had tried his hand. But there are no mooses in the Caribou Country, which is of a very limited area. Of course, wild cats, bears, and perhaps wolves, might be found; yet, that requires time. Therefore all our hunter could do was to "get" his caribou; and then, before the expiration of his leave of absence, hurry after a moose in one of the thirteen counties of the Province where the big elk is still plentiful.

Although our guide was a most experienced and reliable man, he did not wish to undertake the task of leading The Captain to the caribou chase. It takes an Indian to fully understand the ways of this animal. The caribou is different from the European reindeer in size, colour, and habits. A very large American buck, such as those found in Newfoundland, and occasionally in Nova Scotia, will exceed 400 pounds and measure over four feet at the shoulders; thus it presents a much more imposing appearance than the Scandinavian specimen. The American caribou has never been domesticated, and apparently never will be. It is a wanderer *par excellence;* and this is one of the reasons why the white man is often unsuccessful, when hunting without the assistance of an Indian. It is necessary to know exactly the places where the caribou feeds, for the latter is very particular about its diet; it eats mostly lichen, and what is locally called *tripe de roche,* a sort of parasitic lichen growing on the bark of trees. While the moose finds food most anywhere in the forest, and moves only step by step, or even remains often on the same spot—"park"—for weeks at a time, the caribou is frequently compelled to seek new pastures. Besides, it migrates without apparent reason and most unexpectedly; when on the move, it goes on steadily, and does not stop long to eat or to rest, as if in a terrible hurry to reach its destination. Altogether it is an elusive thing, as was soon found out by our Nimrod and the writer—the latter having thought it his duty to accompany the hunting party everywhere.

For several days in succession, we tramped in the vicinity of the camp, through what the Micmac guide described as the normal haunts of our prey—that is to say, a chain of swampy places, to which the wide, loosely connected hoofs of the caribou seem particularly adapted. Several times the Indian assured us that we had come within sight of a buck. We had to take his word for it; although the officer and I prided ourselves on our eyesight, we had not noticed anything. The fact is that the colour of the American caribou—brownish on the legs and shoulders, light grey elsewhere—blends so perfectly with the landscape of that region that, often, only the trained eye of the "native" is apt to distinguish the animal from its background. Each time, the sound of our steps had frightened the game away, in spite of our precautions to wear moccasins. It almost became a habit for us to come back, not only empty handed, but without having fired a shot. The Micmac guide and his white colleague told us that our chances of success were slim, unless a light fall of snow should occur, and enable us to creep, undetected, close to the caribou. But the prospect of a snowstorm did not appeal to the feminine element of the party. Signs of mutiny loomed on the horizon. So it was decided to make a supreme effort! The hunter, the two guides and the writer, equipped in "light marching order," started on a three-day tramp. The weather was misty and chilly, and the "stay at home" ones did not appear to envy us. The Girl's farewell was: "You are sure to bring back something, if not a caribou, at least a cold in the head!"

The Micmac was walking ahead, as a scout; in fact, he was the eyes and the brains of the expedition. The white guide did not

A guide must not only be skilled in the way of the woods but in dealing with the variety of personalities encountered among those entrusted to his care. The Nova Scotia guides employed by the Captain and his party would surely have earned their $3 a day.

THE CAPTAIN AND HIS CARIBOU.

guide at all; he acted as a combination beast of burden, and general information agency.

"The real trouble with this kind of a hunt," remarked The Captain, "is that there is too little left to the white hunter's individuality. He cannot even blame himself if he fails, for everything rests with the Indian scout. All he can do is to defray the expenses of the trip, and act as a shooting machine when brought face to face—without knowing how—with the game. There is not much fun about this! Speak of a wild boar hunt in India! That's life!"

I inquired why no "calling" was resorted to, as in moose-hunting. The white guide replied that caribou-calling was a lost art. Years ago, the Indians knew how to do it: it was a sort of short, hoarse bellow, supposed to imitate the female call. But, apparently, it was not an easy accomplishment to acquire or to teach; and nowadays, while Indians are expert at calling a bull moose, they are unable to do the same for the other animal. Therefore, there is nothing else to do but surprise the game when it is grazing or resting.

At last, the second day, the scout comes upon fresh tracks, and warns us to be extra cautious. This buck is moving at a brisk walk, evidently towards the stream at the bottom of this little vale; we might catch it drinking, but, at the slightest unknown noise, it would change to a long, steady trot, and then we would have no hope of reaching it to-day, for it would not stop for, maybe, an hour or two. To make a long story short, upon reaching the water, by careful and tedious creeping in a single file, we beheld our caribou slowly coming back towards us, a few yards away. The Captain aimed and shot; the buck fell, and all was over in less time than it takes to write this.

The same evening we were back to our base with the head and part of the skin of our "American Reindeer"—and hungry as bears are supposed to be. Were the other members of the party so accustomed to our bad luck that they were disappointed at our success, I could not say. But our return was anything but triumphal. The caribou, or at least its head, was pitied by The Spinster, who declared that The Captain was a heartless being. The Parisian and The Scholar were more anxious to tell us about their fishing at the camp than to listen to our glowing tales of caribou chase. The Girl alone showed us some consideration by preparing for our benefit a porcupine soup, after a recipe she had got from the oldest Micmac woman. For the enlightenment of other tourists, I may mention here that the "porc" is scraped, skinned, the meat is chopped fine, and, with the adjunction of some bones, sliced onions, rice and water, made into a broth. It is not bad. As The Scholar put it, it is neutral. Edith volunteered the information that this recipe was used by Indians and also white sportsmen when other and more respectable meat is getting scarce.

"Thank heavens!" cried her aunt, "we have not come to that yet. Why on earth did you serve us with this awful thing?"

"Gentlemen," tragically stated The Girl, "you may bear witness that each time I am acquiring a new useful accomplishment, I am ruthlessly rebuked."

We did not come back the same way we had reached the Caribou Country, and this for two reasons. First, for the sake of variety, and then because The Captain, before returning to his England station, had time to do some moose-hunting, if he hurried. And, having paid a fee of forty dollars for a big game license of non-resident, he desired to get his money's worth of sports. Therefore, instead of heading for Ingonish and the extreme east shore, we took a southern direction for some thirty-five miles. At Big Intervale we struck a road rather poor, but might have been used by automobile, then, a far better one, at North East Margaree. And finally we made a somewhat imposing and sensational entry into the pretty town of Baddeck, gracefully located on the famous Bras D'Or Lakes. In spite of the late season, we found it well-filled with tourists, mostly

Not all sportsmen who took to the Nova Scotia wilderness were non-residents. Pictured here are Robert Finn, Henry M. (Rosey) Rosenburg, and Harry Russell at Baker's Lake, Halifax County, ca. 1899. Henry Rosenburg was principal of Victoria School of Art and Design in Halifax from 1898 to 1910.

"Americans"—that is to say, from the United States—who, likely, had been detained there by the beauties of the autumn.

At that point, our party broke off temporarily. The hunter went on to Antigonish, a queer Scottish settlement, from where he intended to reach the Guysboro district, which, he had been told, was the nearest place for moose-hunting. The Spinster, who generally did the unexpected, left by a small coastal steamer to visit the rugged shore as far as Cape North, that with Cape Smoky—whose top is more often than not concealed by mist—had a powerful attraction for her romantic imagination. The Parisian, of course, could not fail to take advantage of the pause in our journey to see Louisbourg, the old French citadel that played so important a part in the long tragedy ended by the fall of Quebec. But neither The Girl, nor The Scholar, nor the writer deemed it worth while to leave cozy, peaceful Baddeck and the shady lawns of the New Bras D'Or Hotel—a welcome contrast to the stern nature of the Caribou Country.

DR. EDDIE BRECK

American sportsman, writer, scholar, and diplomat, 1914

Dan Jack Murray, head guide for Eddie Breck's trip to the Cape Breton caribou grounds.

I would like to say that the man who penetrates to the caribou grounds of Cape Breton by way of the Northwest Margaree River once may claim to be something of a hero; but the man who tried it the second time would be a fit subject for an alienist. There are caribou on Cape Breton. I am going to tell you about one or two that we saw and describe how we hunted, plus the experiences of my friends. I may not always stick strictly to continuity of events, but what you want is a real idea of how the thing is done.

My good friend, Chief Game Commissioner Knight of Nova Scotia, was familiar with the caribou grounds of Victoria, one of the only two counties where there is now an open season for caribou, going in from Ingonish on the eastern coast. But he was interested in discovering a way to reach the country from the west side of the island, and therefore placed me in communication with Game Warden Ross of North East Margaree, a settlement on the salmon-angling branch of that beautiful river, who held out the most roseate promises in regard to game, country, and guides. It was therefore with high hopes that I journeyed to the little mining town of Inverness, by way of the Dominion Atlantic and Intercolonial lines of railway. I am glad I went to the caribou grounds the wrong way, for I thus discovered a paradise, namely, the valley of the Margaree, especially from the forks up the N.E. Branch, which, it would seem, must be the best salmon river in Nova Scotia, to say nothing of sea trout. In any case handsome it is, running serenely through the broad green valley, dotted with splendid elms and surrounded by high hills, almost mountains. This branch has its rise not in any lake, but is the agglomeration of countless little brooks that dash down from the springs of the barren above, and the water is as clear as crystal. No wonder the salmon like it. And how canny the salmon anglers are! Hardly a word do you hear about the Margaree nowadays. The best pools are quietly taken up by a few astute fishermen from outside who come every year. As for single self, I am going up there next June, and I am going to stop with the postmistress, Mrs. Ross, who keeps a deliciously clean little inn, and I am going to have the time of my life up that N.E. Branch, landing sea trout of two to six pounds in weight! I say nothing about the salmon; that's of course.

But to return to our caribou. It is over twenty miles from Inverness to Mrs. Ross', and thence farther up the valley eleven miles to Kingross, represented, so far as I could see, by three houses, one of them, the "farthest north," being inhabited by Dan Murray, the one licensed guide of all that region. But Dan was not at home, as the warden had got things a bit mixed and we were not expected until Monday, this being Saturday. Inadvertently I mentioned starting on the morrow, whereupon Mrs. Murray gave me a look that would have killed a duck at fifty yards and said something about the people round about being good Christians, and she hoped she never would see her man goin' off with a pack on his back on a Sabbath, no, she certainly hoped she never would live to see that! And the few natives who had gathered round to have a look at the hardy caribou-hunter shook their heads ominously. Of course I hastened to assure Mrs. Murray that I had not stopped to think that to-morrow was Sunday, but, though she softened somewhat, I got the distinct impression that I was "in bad" with the guide wife.

Monday, early, we again put in an appearance at Kingross, and there was at once a great powwow concerning the provisions and other impedimenta, for I had brought three pack-baskets full, a sleeping-bag, and other such stuff having no idea in the world of the journey ahead of me. In the lake country of Nova Scotia we are not accustomed to count the pounds very carefully, as the portages are short and one doesn't mind a heavy load for a short distance on the level. But these strapping Highlanders shook their heads to such an extent that I began to be frightened, with the result that we started with all the heavy stuff, such as canned goods, left behind, including my whole extra clothing outfit except one suit of underwear and a couple of handkerchiefs. My sole foot-covering consisted of a pair of hunting shoes, which, though excellent in their way, were a trifle heavy for the kind of work before us.

Finally we made our start up the picturesque valley, which narrows here, the river plunging down at a great rate over the stones. I have never felt so much like the head of an African safari in my life, for no fewer than five men accompanied me, each with a pack on his back. There was Dan himself, who complained of rheumatism and carried a rather light burden, shedding a lurid light on his make-up. Then came "little Dan" (Donald) Ross and his son Willie, a husky boy with a good outlook as a future guide, and big Neil McLeod, who, with a claymore in his hand and the kilts of his ancestors flying in the wind, might have frightened a Lowlander into fits in the Forty-Five, but who was the mildest, most good-natured chap in the world, and a fellow of infinite jest. Demure Torquil Stewart was the last.

A carry is meant to be the shortest distance between two given places and it doesn't strive for luxury.... It will skin along the sharp edge of slippery rocks set up at impossible angles, so that only a mountain goat can follow it without risking his neck. I believe it would climb a tree if a big one stood directly in its path. Albert Bigelow Paine, 1905

The first two hours were consumed in ascending the valley, often wading the shores and twice crossing the stream in primitive board skiffs. Much of the walking was over rocks, slippery with wet moss, and, with the packs on our backs, it was no gentle saunter. My shoes were not new and were worn rather smooth, and it required some skill to keep my balance. Is there anything more disconcerting or, for the matter of that, more severely trying to muscles and temper, than to slip and lose one's balance while carrying a heavy pack? The jolting strain that invariably follows takes it out of one more than a couple of miles of going on the level. I was not exactly soft, but I had been living for a fortnight in those unwholesome things called houses, and this start was not soothing to my nerves. I had on my back my sleeping-bag, with some other things inside, and my knapsack on top of that, with a camera slung over my shoulder and my .35 in my hands. It might have weighed altogether between forty-five and fifty pounds. The others, except Dan, carried as much or more.

At last we left the valley of the main river, after Dan had pointed out a bold bluff towering half a mile right above us, with the remark that "There's where we go up!" Following along a little brook for a mile or so, we at last began to go upwards. And believe me, my friends, it was upwards! Narrower and steeper and wetter grew the gorge until it was a steep gulch with a brook trickling down or oozing out of it. We were a good deal over an hour getting up the last steep incline, often so precipitous that both hands were needed to pull one's self up. And how slippery the moss was, and how my back ached, and how I sweated! We rested every fifty yards or less, for often it was a sheer upwards climb. The others were palpably tired—that was my only consolation—and there was very little conversation as we sat puffing during the rests. As for myself, I must confess that my 135 pounds were very nearly unequal to the task of my pack, and I went up that mountain gorge on my nerve alone.

About half-way up, during one of the pauses, I took off my knapsack, which rested badly on the top of my pack, intending to tie it on more securely. But when we were ready to start again I missed the sack, and a glance showed me that little Donald Ross had quietly slung it over his shoulder. For a moment pride struggled with common sense, finally to succumb. Little Dan wobbled sadly up the incline with that top-heavy knapsack falling one way and then the other, but never complaining. When at last we reached the summit I thanked him and demanded the sack back. To my surprise he took it off and passed it over with a distinct sigh of relief. Dan doubtless had all he cared to lug already, but fancy one of my Annapolis County boys giving up anything in the pack line to his sportsman! Nevertheless, little Dan is no "quitter," quite the contrary. He is merely inexperienced in the art of guiding, as are the rest. I speedily found that, if I wanted anything, I had to ask for it. The anticipation of an employer's needs was unknown to these men, though they had the kindest hearts in the world. It was amusing to see five husky men

The inexperienced may imagine—not even the enthusiast can fully comprehend until he has actually enjoyed it—the pleasure of sitting round the camp-fire after a good day's work, and a hearty supper, and chatting in that easy unforced way, which one seldom can follow when under the shadow of more critical ears. And should you be more wakeful than your companions, and sit later than they, you will find your solitude broken in upon by those grand mysterious noises in the woods at night, which make, to a vivid fancy, the forest seem as an enchanted land. Away in the great darkness, in the circle beyond the little cosy arena reddened and glowing with our merry fire, one hears every now and then—all as if intensified by the solitude and the darkness—the crash of some falling tree, the melancholy note of the owl as he sits "warming his five wits," or the wail of the loon by some small forest lake.

Francis Duncan, 1864

standing round and nobody with any idea what to do; and it was not until the last of the trip that each man took up his allotted task without being told to do it. A lean-to-tent, to my mind the only tent in any weather but the coldest of winter, they had never seen, but mine was appreciated when the big camp-fire roared before it on a coolish evening.

Once upon the high plateau that extends pretty nearly all over the northern part of the interior of Cape Breton, we began to notice signs of game, hitherto only a "partridge" or two being seen. Especially were evidences of foxes very common, and hawks, particularly Cooper's, flew about everywhere. The island is separated from the rest of Nova Scotia only by a mile or so of water, and yet the differences in the fauna are marked. That ubiquitous, destructive, good-for-nothing, delightfully awkward and curious beast, the porcupine, is unknown on Cape Breton, and so, too, are the skunk and the wildcat. On the other hand, the marten and Canada lynx (one lynk, two lynks, is the way the woodsmen put it), unknown in Nova Scotia, are common here. The moose they have killed off, and the bear are few. Worth mentioning is a (to me at least) new name for the already much-named Canada jay, which the guides called the "carron jay," a designation for which they could give no reason. Very likely *carrion* is meant.

That first night I shall not soon forget. The men, being used to crawling into their stove-heated trapping cabins, had no bedding, the result being that all hands spent the cold night hours in keeping up the big fire, often using the ax, which is not conducive to gentle slumber. They also talked and sang, and, judging from certain significant noises, had a bite to eat now and then. It apparently never occurred to them that their employer might possibly care for a wink or two of sleep. I wouldn't have minded it so much if the concert and conversation had been carried on in English, but among themselves these second and third generation Highlanders invariably speak Gaelic, and my brain got so interested, in spite of myself, in trying to make out, from the few Gaelic words I knew, what they were saying, that slumber quite fled from me. Under October 7 I read in my notebook: "Hellova night. Dan champion talker; Neil champion singer. For a few minutes somebody must have slept, for he snored like the trombones in the introduction to the third act of 'Lohengrin.' "

Incidentally during this hunt I was reminded forcibly of the difference between the Lowland and Highland Scotch and their languages. The first day I tried a little "broad" Scotch that I had picked up from professional golf-teachers on Dan, but he stared for a moment and then remarked, "Ah, that will be Lowland talk, I think." When these Highlanders use English they speak it like you or me.

No wonder a very sleepy band of men started on the trail next morning. I had flattered myself that our pedestrian trails were over, but I was mistaken, for the walking up there was bad. All my life long I have longed to wander in a genuine virgin, totally unlumbered forest, and this wish was now gratified, though my esthetic sense was not. No giant pines and spruces here, though there were trees enough of this kind, the tallest being hardly over fifty feet in height. For firewood we felled a couple of birches, and Dan showed me the rings in the wood, which became so thick and numerous near the bark that it was impossible to count them.

Dan opined that many of these spruces and white birches were hundreds of years old, and declared that, to his knowledge, one of them on this plateau will not grow over an inch a year. The reasons for this are that the soil is too shallow above the pre-Cambrian bedrock and the winds buffet the woods very grievously. As a result the thick woods are quite covered with windfalls ("blow-downs," the natives call them), and with scrub growth of every kind, the worst being the firs, spruces and the maples, the latter sending out their tough branches horizontally along the ground like snakes turned to wood, as if with the intention of tripping the feet of the unwary traveler.

Add to this condition of things that, since the country has never been visited by lumbermen (these fell gentry destroy only the beautiful forests!), there are no tote-roads or paths of any kind except those of the caribou from barren to barren, and that the barrens, or muskegs, are mostly covered with soft moss into which the feet sink over the ankles and often to the knees, and it is easy to see that there is little rest for the weary in this God-forsaken region. More than that, the many brooks all rise here and, in descending to the plains, form deep gulches that must be crossed, so that progression is apt to be a good deal up and down.

At this time of year the caribou are in the green woods, and the natives do not hunt them until snow comes and the animals come out on the barrens to feed on the white moss. In October practically the only way to hunt them is to intercept them while using their paths from one piece of woods to another across the barrens.

Interior of unidentified camp ca. 1900.

Nevertheless, it seemed proper to stick to the barrens, since the woods were so thick as to make still-hunting next to impossible, and we made directly for the great Cape North Barren, one of the most extensive on the island, in the hope that there, if anywhere at this season, we should see

caribou. It was a three days' hike thither, and the only party that reached there before me had left its sentiments written on a tree at Dan's camp, where we spent the second night. It was in the form of a "poem," and ran thus:

> *"We whose names are here appended,*
> *Our weary way to the barrens wended.*
> *We damn well wish we were back home,*
> *This cursed trail ne'er more to roam!"*

Dan's cabins were of logs covered with birch-bark, which is very plentiful here, there having been no canoes to build.

It was a relief when at last Dan and I were able to start out without being weighted down with packs, and we covered the three miles from the last camp to the big barren in short order. There is always a measure of excitement on reaching a barren or other clearing, as there may be caribou on it. The method is to approach from leeward and scan the country with a glass from the last cover on the edge. Tracks we found, but nothing very fresh, and even the great barren failed to show us a moving thing, though we wandered over it for miles, and had a clear view for a long distance in every direction. Even the hills on the coast, both east and west, were visible. We therefore "boiled the kettle" while Dan regaled me with his choicest whoppers, in which the bull caribou were always killed and never bore less than thirty or forty points.

For the afternoon Dan had reserved a part of the barren that stretched away toward the north with a gentle dip that concealed it from the highest knoll when we had scanned the region. At the bottom of this slope was a grassy valley spotted with small, tarnlike ponds, the only vegetation being clumps of scrub growth. To within a quarter of a mile from these tarns ran a tract of scrub spruces, so low that we were obliged to stoop in order to get any cover. We would advance through this for fifty yards or less and then pause to scrutinize the valley in front. During one of these pauses came our first thrill. Dan had scarcely taken up the glass when he exclaimed: "I see two lyin' down by that bunch o' scrub! They're bulls! Look!" And he handed me the glass.

Sure enough, I could distinctly see two brilliant spots of white, which Dan said were the necks of the caribou. "Come!" he said in a low voice, and we started off toward the quarry, moving swiftly through the scrub with a low stoop, often, indeed, on hands and knees, where the cover was sparse. Every once in a while we would stop and examine the animals through the glass, and it seemed to me that they moved about somewhat, but Dan said they were only moving their heads. There were still at least a hundred yards to cover before we could think of shooting, and we gradually made about this distance with the greatest care.

"Can't you see their horns?" inquired Dan anxiously. I had to confess my inability to distinguish any antlers, though we were not within shot, but it seemed to me that there were more than two caribou, or at least white spots.

"When we fire, Doctor, you take the right-hand one, and I'll take the left!" whispered Dan. It had been decided that Dan should also kill a bull if he had the chance, since he was entitled to one, and could use the smoked meat later while trapping, thus saving a strenuous lug of meat up the mountain.

We gained another twenty or thirty yards, and it appeared to me that, if there were any antlers worth having, they ought now to be in evidence. Suddenly I whispered: "Look here, Dan, there are five of them, whatever they are!"

Dan took a careful look with the glass. I could feel his shoulder tremble slightly as it touched mine, and I remember warming to him for this great interest, which amounted to real sporting excitement. I had my rifle cocked and ready to fire if the caribou jumped, and I wondered that Dan took such a long look. I saw him scowl, then look again very intently. At last he let the glass fall and gazed at me with a curious expression on his face.

"Yes, you're right!" he said in a voice of mourning. "There's five of 'em, all right, but they're wild geese!"

It was one of those moments when conflicting emotions come together like the warring currents where three streams run into one. But disappointment and disgust soon gave way to a sense of the ridiculous, and we both burst out laughing over this very literal wild-goose chase. The geese heard our guffaws and started to walk away in a very dignified manner. As for Dan and me, we returned to camp in a rather crestfallen state of mind.

Next day I proceeded to put a plan into operation from which I expected results, if results were obtainable at that season. It was to take my sleeping-bag and spend the night on the Cape North Barren, and thus be on hand if the caribou came out either at eve or early morning, or crossed at those times on their way to other parts of the woods. Accordingly Dan and Donald helped me take my stuff to the barren, and left me there in time to get back to their camp before nightfall. I spread the bag in a clump of scrub spruces, with a light tarpaulin spread over it on two sticks, and collected dry stuff enough for a little fire, the kettle having been filled at a brook on our way to the barren.

The guides were loth to leave me so, but I was but carrying out an old theory—that the best still-hunting party consists of one man, the next best of two, and so forth. A single man's attention is not taken up by his companion, so that he gives it all to the matter in hand. He therefore hears and sees more, and makes far less noise than if in company. After taking a turn round the highest knoll on the barren, and convincing myself that nothing living bigger than a hare was

Tales such as the 'Wild Goose Chase' made great table fare among sports and guides at the end of day.

within miles of me, I made myself a cup of cocoa, ate my piece of bread and butter and cold bacon, and turned in.

What a wondrous night that was! The moon was nearly full, and there were stars too, and the temperature fell to far below the freezing point. Deep silence brooded over the face of the earth, made still deeper by the occasional hoot of an owl or the bark of a fox. Once a hare nearly ran over my bed, and scurried off in a panic when it discovered my whereabouts. A heavy dew fell and froze on my bedding, so that when, just before daybreak, I crawled out of my bag, I had to be very careful not to break the canvas, which was stiff and white with hoarfrost. The water in kettle and cup was frozen solid, and it was shivery work until I got a fire going and a cup of hot coffee "next my heart." I was on the barren in time to see the sun come up in splendor and drench the earth with the melted frost.

By the time Dan arrived I had convinced myself that nary caribou was within scouting distance, and we turned sadly back toward camp. But there was still a good chance left, for on the way lay several smaller barrens linked by strips of second-growth woods, and these we followed, finding some fresh tracks on the old caribou paths. We also found something else which was both significant and ominous, namely, the remains of a caribou snare, consisting of two uprights, one on each side of the path, at a point where the animals were practically sure to pass through, a big tree which had evidently served as a spring-pole, and a kind of paddle-shaped piece of hewn wood about thirty inches long, with a small, square hole in it. This was designed for the doomed beast to place its feet upon, the heavy noose of rope then jerking it up to a position in which it was quite helpless, a more or less lingering death being the result.

The guides said there had been no snaring for many years, but these remnants did not look so very old. There used to be vast herds of caribou in this region. Possibly the art of snaring has something to do with their diminution. *Absit omen!*

Dan asserted that he had often approached caribou from the windward, but Dan is given to spinning yarns, and I took notice that on this occasion, when he was really anxious to score, we circled the first muskeg very carefully until we could cross near a likely looking second-growth "neck o' woods" that reached out into the bog like a point, without throwing our scent in that direction. There was an unusual amount of small growth on the barren, which also undulated in surface more than most others, and Dan never moved farther than thirty yards without subjecting the landscape to a long and thorough scrutiny with the glass, which he would then pass to me with the request to do likewise. We had been following, for some time since we left the big barren, the tracks of a small herd, among which were those of a good-sized bull, when suddenly the spoor turned off toward the left down a swale. Here was where the guide's knowledge of the country came in, as it usually does, with telling effect.

"They'll follow that for a mile and then turn back to the Third Branch barren," he said. "That's right over there. If we are not too late we may meet them. The bull has been following the cows, and if he gets up to 'em they may go slower or stop entirely. Come on fast now." And he set a quick pace across the narrow neck o' woods that might be masking our quarry.

A sacrifice to Diana and a candle to Saint Hubert! Luck was with us, for, as we paused in the underbrush on the barren's edge, we made out the brown-and-white figures of half a dozen wood-land caribou on the other side, about two hundred yards distant. Dan handed the glass to me.

"Them ain't no geese this time!" he whispered. "I make out one good bull anyway."

I examined the little herd with beating heart (shall I ever get blasé when game appears?) and agreed that there was a shootable bull over there, though perhaps no record head. Carefully choosing our way, we started to creep across the barren toward the group, which was feeding quietly. The scrub growth, the wind in our faces, and the undulations of the ground surface made the stalk a fairly easy one, and at last I maneuvered myself into a position from which, lying nearly prone with a rest over a dead spruce stump, I covered the herd at less than one hundred yards. As there was only one large bull Dan decided not to fire, but held himself ready to do so if the bull showed signs of getting away, a thing hardly possible at that distance with a steady rest for the powerful .35.

As usual, a great calm came over me as I aimed, and at the mighty bang the bull reared slightly, then swayed and fell on his side, only to struggle to his feet. It was easy to see that he was hard hit, but every second of suffering is agony for a true sportsman, and a second shot put the great deer down for good. The hunt was over.

I lost five pounds on that trip. Next time I shall follow Mr. Knight's advice and go in from the eastern side, for I feel a good deal like a friend who was getting bald and who dreaded to go to the barber's. "Every time I go," he said, "I lose a hair, and I can't afford that!"

CHAPTER 6

SUMMER DAYS ON A NOVA SCOTIAN SALMON STREAM

ARTHUR P. SILVER

well known Halifax sports- man and writer, 1907

It is a Nova Scotian stream of which I am writing, and like many oth- ers of that province it has its birthplace—its cradle so to speak—in one of those numerous lake basins which are sprinkled over the interior in countless number, and a short course of some twenty miles to the Atlantic seaboard. The lower portion of the stream, a strip of some three miles, offers the best fishing, and only lately seventeen fish have been hooked in one day in this stretch of water. It affords a choice of some eleven good pools.

In this part of the fishing world one meets on almost every river an Admiral's pool, a General's pool, a Priest's, and a Doctor's. The titles are all reminiscent of worthies not unforgotten among the angling fra- ternity; 'good anglers now with God' would have been Walton's com- ment on all of them, had he known and loved them as many out here have done—'men of mild, sweet and peaceable spirits such as most anglers have.' Other resting stations of the salmon are: the 'Pet Pool,' where the river gathers its waters into an oily smoothness in a narrow

I know of no other pastime or field sport, a love of which once acquired, that gives such lasting and perfect enjoyment as fly-fishing.

Edward Samuels, 1890

funnel before it plunges into a wild rapid, where many a good fish severs his connexion with the rod; the 'Hemlock Pool,' where a large tree of that species deepens the darkness of the already dark water with its feathery branches; the 'Oak Pool,' where, beneath deep shadows of leafage in the turf-cushioned arm-chairs made by massive twisting roots, many an honest fisherman has eaten his midday sandwich and washed it down with a cool draught from the adjacent 'whiskey spring'; the 'Still Pool,' the cast of a fisherman, which must be made with the smallest of flies, gently as an autumn leaf fluttered by a faint breeze on the water, where a brown strip of submerged rock marks the chosen 'seat' of many a fine fish; the 'Flat Rock,' and 'The Turn,' and 'Fool's Pool,' and 'Rocky,' and 'The Meadow,' and the 'Champagne,' with its creamy bubbling water; and the 'Foot of the Lake,' and 'Log Pool,' and 'The Dam.' Is not the reason for each memory of each one a delight on nights when the path to the salmon pool is deep in snow and the pool itself sleeping beneath its coverlet of ice?

A sudden swerve of the highway, and there is the river—glimmering, dancing, sparkling along its boulder-strewn channel, racing right merrily to swift annihilation in the tiny harbour, which twists stealthily in from the sea. We draw rein as we reach the little bridge with its wooden piers fretting the impetuous current, and look outwards on the blue salt water dotted with tawny sails of fishing boats; at the white cottages of fishermen sprinkled along the shores; at the background of dark fir trees, whose barbed tops on the one side are traced as in India-ink against a cloudless sky, and on the other are burnt and bitten into a fiery sunset. It is the view up the valley threaded by the little salmon stream we have come hither to fish which more steadfastly holds my gaze. Swiftly towards me, between serried ranks of coniferous trees embroidered with the white stems of silver birches, now with loud murmurings, now with soft musical purl, again fairly shouting among the grey granite boulders, which are strewn on its pathway, sometimes slow slipping over golden pebbles, sometimes swift sliding over glassy ledges, comes my fascinating friend—the river.

For friend and companion for the next two weeks this river is to be to me. At night its voice will soothe me deliciously; all day long I will draw its cheerful life into my veins. I will study its moods. There may arise forbidding moods; but, like some capricious charmer after spent anger rewarding her patient lover with an unforgettable smile, there is sure to come at length the sudden swift unveiling of dazzling divine beauty. It may be a sunset-hour after rain, when there unfolds a sudden transformation into an atmosphere so clear, so marvellous, so brilliant, that the passage of light on the river (which is the imperishable heart of the scene) glorifies the whole landscape, until it becomes transfigured with colours never caught on the canvas of Titian or of Turner.

On the bridge stands Enoch, my guide, gaff in hand, a true son of the forest. Sixty winters have not grizzled the heavy mass of brown hair on his face and head, though his body is twisted with the wet and cold. 'Uncle Enoch' the village imps call him, wondering, with little arms akimbo as he returns from the river, how many salmon are hid within the leather bag at his side to give his shoulders that unwonted stoop. He wears a drab woollen shirt, open at the neck, half revealing his swarthy breast, and a gift suit of chequered Harris tweed, at least one size too small, so that his lean muscular arms, knotted like whipcords and burned to a brown-black by the summer

Uncle Enoch running the rapids. "Here's to the guide, so faithful and true, when he gets in rough water he knows what to do; We have faith in him always and truly pray, he will guide us back safely, for he knows the way."

Herbert Allan Leslie

suns, are exposed almost to the elbow. Nature's elemental forces—winds, rains, sun, frost—have made the features of the man too weather-worn and rigid for emotional expression, save that one can notice a somewhat contemptuous upward curl in the corners of the mouth if a fish is handled without due skill or the pool has not been covered in orthodox fashion. A quiet taciturn man is Enoch, as if he knew that a sportsman's first duty was stealthiness and his second silence. A true sportsman, too, most thorough in all his methods.

"Throw out there in the bubbly water and kiver the whole pool, sir," is his laconic message, when he notices that I am missing a likely looking eddy, where a whirl or two in the sable water marking sunken boulders, which lure a salmon to rest, seem to him to be escaping the searching sweep of my Silver Doctor; and always Uncle Enoch is quite right. On the particular occasion here recalled, as the No. 2 Doctor swings round above the curl of the wave that plays at the head of the riff, there comes an upheaval of water dear to the angler's eye, and the back fin and pink side of a large salmon are revealed, but quickly curtained by the closing flood. A few moments to rest him—and perhaps there are no more delicious moments in the angler's experience, only to be compared to the delight of putting together the rod for the first time after the long sleep of winter—and I send the fly inch by inch nearer to where he broke, on the tiptoe of expectation. But no response. Surely my friend has gotten a taste of its quality? What can be wrong?

"Perhaps he has moved, sir; kiver all the pool, sir, if you please," says good old Enoch.

Acting on the suggestion I lengthen my line and send a cast several yards away to the other side of the ripple from the rock. The response is immediate; with a sidelong rush that shows his black back and gleaming sides the salmon seizes the fly, and instantly the line begins to hiss from the reel, while the rod is strained almost double. My friend proves a very game fish of nearly twenty pounds and evidently set a high estimate on the value of his life, for he fought long and valiantly, and left no tactics untried to rid himself of the toils. A series of high springs, a straightway rush at the pace of ninety miles an hour, electric twistings under water, jerking savagely, and striking heavily at the leader with his tail—all proved of no avail. Admiration for his pluck almost made me regret his fate, but Enoch's relentless gaff quivered for one moment only above his victim, then instantly with unerring aim the bright steel was buried in the shining side, and the metallic body was laid bright and beautiful amid the rushy sedges on the shelving shore. Here indeed was a good fish, saved that but for Enoch's vigilance, I might never have made acquaintance with. 'Kiver the whole pool' is an excellent axiom when you angle for a salmon.

Enoch on occasion is good at a yarn, and as we sit in the shade enjoying the afternoon pipe he loves to recall stories of 'the Old Hunter,' a retired colonel who once fished this river with a very long rod (18 ft.), bearing inverse ratio to the quality of his temper. "Rest his soul, he's dead and gone; he was the best sportsman as ever fished in these parts," was Enoch's epigrammatic verdict on him who proved Walton's rule concerning the peaceable mild spirits of anglers by affording a most notable exception.

Sportsman General Chambers McKibbin visited Milford House, Annapolis County, regularly in the early 1900s. With his stoic appearance, and his reputed ability to "curse well," he could easily pass for Enoch's "choleric Colonel."

"Onc't," continued Enoch, "he was wexed by a sportsman casting into his water from the opposite bank. He said nothing, but managed to cross the man's line and tied it to the bushes. Didn't it sarve the man right? Onc't he thrashed two Indians within an inch of their lives for stealing a jug of old Jamaica rum *cachéd* at one of his camps for winter moose-hunting. Another man annoyed him by unlawful fishing. He found out where the critter hid his spears and dip-nets and other things that are a hurt to the river. One day he found a fifty-fathom net with a leader, besides spears and bags and triangles. Lord, it was wild! And the Colonel he gets wild too, and goes to a magistrate and slaps the fine on him. But that did no good. So the next time he found this man poaching he took off his coat, for he had wexed him too bad this time to stand it any further. Instead of slapping on the fine this time, he says to the poacher, 'If we have a law let it be a law, and we must fight it out betwixt us right here and now.' The man was a shocking big brute of a fellow, but did not stand up for long before the Colonel; after three rounds he was on the ground howling with pain. He limped home to his wife—very badly hurt, they told me—and ever after the Colonel had no trouble on that river when they knew he was out for his sport. Onc't he fit a duel in Halifax because some big man sent a favourite rod back he had loaned him with a broken tip."

So with yarns of the choleric Colonel did Enoch beguile the hour of siesta one bright afternoon as we smoked our pipes, resting on the slope of the mill-dam, whence we had a view of the Falls Pool immediately beneath us. It is a good pool, but full of sunken logs and branches, which a hooked fish is not slow to take advantage of. Indeed, it is one of those pools that afford so many chagrins that I would not advise a man of 'mild and peaceable spirit' to fish it too often, lest he might fall from grace and develop a temper. *Crede experto.* The way of a salmon among submerged timber passeth all understanding.

It is a curious pool to fish, for you cast from the dam, and as you look down upon the sunny water you often see a fish or two sculling gently along with a dreamy motion, or else poised at his station on easy fin. You can see the whole process of his taking the fly, and are very apt to draw it away on that account before your fish has well seized it. Personally, I prefer not to see the fish for which I cast, as I much enjoy that sudden revelation of what lurks behind the veil—the quick surprise, the lifting of the curtain that hides the finny tribe from observation.

Our river distinctly divides itself into three parts: the upper is infancy, the middle is youth, the lower manhood. The upper reach is where the waters are gathered into a large lacustrine expansion swelled by numberless small rivulets teeming with parr and with trout, big and little; in its middle course the stream gathers strength until it affords a few fair pools where one can take grilse in midsummer. But it is to the lower reach that memory turns most often in other scenes than these, for here is our battle-ground with *Salmo salar,*

Two unidentified sports stand in front of Milford House before embarking upon a fishing trip into the back-country. It was common in the early 1900s for families to spend the entire summer season at hotels, tourist homes, and private clubs scattered around the province. This trend changed following World War II as tourism took on a more transient look and guiding began to lose its lustre.

here are registered our victories and defeats.

What a lovely pool is Indian Camp! Quite near the sloping green bank old Indian warriors lie at rest beneath a score of fern-clad mounds; men who long ago fished here with their rude gear and made elaborate stone weirs, traces of which are still to be seen, notably in the Weir Pool. It is only a stone's-throw above tidal water, and when the salmon rise here they come savagely, with tiger-like spring, apparently more strong and lusty than after they have lived in the fresh water even for a little time. Then succeeds 'The Alders,' where brown tassels and metallic leafage dip in a sable reach of water flecked with foam bells, netting among their interlacing branches frothy fabrics like pyramids of whipped cream.

Next come the Lower and Upper Wing-dams, salmon pools of great interest to the fisherman, for in reality they are artificial pools, not made for the angler's delight expressly, but incidentally serving his purpose. They are structures built by the lumbermen for facilitating the driving of logs, provided with a gate in the centre, and with sides set sloping to the stream, furnishing a sort of funnel or bottle-neck pool, and backing up the water to a depth which the salmon dearly loves— anywhere between two and three feet—and somehow correcting the speed of the current exactly to his taste. Should any reader wish to construct an artificial salmon pool here is a valuable model, for above these so-called 'wing-dams' the salmon will surely rest for a long time. A fish hooked and lost here on June 12 of last year was taken with the cast in his jaws by another fisherman at exactly the same spot on June 27. He had remained in the pool for all that time.

For two whole weeks this pleasing river had been to me companion and friend. Life by its waters had bestowed the power to enjoy simple things. 'The gliding of the stream, and the birds singing, and the soft blue sky, seem like life passing in a summer dream, as though no winter stress could e'er come nigh a scene like this, or any human deeds seem louder than the whisper of the reeds.' Oh, happy state of mind, when mere sky and running water, rocks and trees, the fluttering leafage, the glory of a summer eve, the notes of birds from the tree-tops, can make one forget that life holds anything save rapture in it. As I pause at the top of the hill overlooking the river, tracing my steps backwards towards the ties of humanity, which for awhile have been almost completely severed, I find myself repeating these words, hardly exaggerated, though originally referred to human love:

Now see,
The red sun drops behind the dusky hills,
And nightly dews rise from the sombre vale:
Farewell, beloved, for belov'd thou art.

CHAPTER 7

A FISHING LESSON

Next to killing a good fish myself, I love to see a friend take one, and I can honestly asseverate that I have, time and again, had more pleasure in helping a comrade to a royal fish, than I should have had if it had fallen to my own rod. It is only a 'fish hog' who wants it all himself. Yes, there's nothing like a fishing trip with a man to show his true character. I remember an incident that will illustrate this.

I was once fishing a river in Nova Scotia with a man whom I had always considered a perfect type of a gentleman, but inside of three days he exhibited traits that I would not have supposed he possessed. We were stopping at the same hotel, and had the river all to ourselves. At the beginning we agreed to draw lots for pools, and it being my first choice, I took the first pool from the salt water, he the second, I the third, and so on through the whole five miles of fishing that we had. I noticed that his countenance seemed to show dissatisfaction when the choices were made, but as nothing could possibly be fairer than our arrangement, I took no notice of his discomfort. He had fully as good pools as I had, and I could think of no more equitable way of dividing them.

Well, our first day on the river was one to be remembered. We left the hotel together and walked to the river, a mile or so, chatting pleasantly and enjoying the delightful morning hugely. But when we reached the river, and I began rigging for my first cast in my pool, instead of going along to his own, he sat down on a log and began grumbling like a bear with a sore head.

"It's just my infernal luck," he said, "to have you get this pool. I always liked it, and in fact it's a favorite with me."

"Well," I said to him, "I don't mind; you take my pools and I'll take yours to-day, and to-morrow we will change."

"No," replied my friend, "that will give you the fourth pool to-day, and as that is the best pool on the river, and it has not been fished lately, I am sure of a salmon in it."

"Very good," I answered, "we'll stick to the original program."

By this time I was rigged and ready to begin casting. My friend still sat on his log, although I suggested he had better take advantage of the early fishing. I began casting, and rose a beautiful fish at the third cast. I missed him, and then such a growl as my companion uttered would have tried the patience of Job.

"Just my infernal luck. Oh! what a beautiful fish. If I had had this pool. Cuss the luck, " etc., etc.

I waited a few minutes and then began casting again, and soon rose and hooked my salmon. It was a bright silvery fish just from the sea. Such a look of absolutely green jealousy and envy as I caught on the face of my friend, I had never seen before, and it destroyed all the pleasure I was expecting. However, I played the fish as well as I could, but I felt nervous, for I had never before had such an experience. Alas, my casting line parted in the middle of one of the furious runs of the salmon, and he was free.

"Too bad, too bad," exclaimed my friend, but his countenance belied his words, for if ever I saw a face lighted up with satisfaction, his was.

He took his rod and guide and started off

I caught forty-eight salmon in the Musquodoboit River. Had ten days leave from my regiment. I took one day to journey there and another to return, Sunday of course was not a fishing day; consequently I had only seven clear days fishing. The fish with one or two exceptions were brought to Leonard Gaetz's House. I lost at least thirty of a good size; all captured were full sized. One fish weighed by Mr. Crawford proved to be 33 lbs. weight. The second morning, being alone, I captured six salmon before breakfast time eight o'clock....

William Chearnley, 1839

for the second pool. After repairing damages—the fault was in the
casting line, a flat place only an inch in length in the gut having broken, all the rest of the leader being perfect—I cast in the same pool
again for a while, but without any success. At length I reeled up, and
with my guide moved along up to the third pool, which was my next
one. As we passed the second my friend was busy casting, but he had

had no rises, as his guide informed us.

At the third pool at my second cast I hooked and killed a grilse, and soon after rose a fine salmon, hooked and played him, and my guide was just on the point of gaffing the fish when my friend joined us. He came down the path with a bound, and as we killed the salmon he burst out with a loud, "I congratulate you; I congratulate you!" but he looked ready to cry. All this made me so uncomfortable that I said I would give him the balance of the river for the day, for I had had all the fishing I wanted, and with my guide carrying my salmon and grilse, I returned to the hotel.

Well the next day it was the same story, and the next. Nothing would satisfy him, and on the evening of the third day, I told him that on the next morning I was going to another river a few miles away, and he would have this stream all to himself, and even that did not satisfy him, for his last words when I left him on the following day were: "Don't kill all the salmon in the river, for I expect to fish it in a few days."

Yes, there is nothing like going fishing with a man to give one a true insight into his character.

CHAPTER 8

EDWARD A.
SAMUELS
American
sportsman, 1890

ON THE MARGAREE

The tourist, as well as fisherman, will find much to interest and delight him in a visit to Cape Breton. It abounds in picturesque scenery, and some of the views that one may have there are really magnificent. In leaving Boston the tourist has a choice between three steamer routes and two by rail. One steamer leaves on Saturdays, and touches at Halifax and other points on the Nova Scotia coast, and lands you at Port Hawksbury. Another runs to Annapolis, from which point there is a railroad to Port Mulgrave. The third steamer belonging to the International Steamship Company will carry you direct to St. John, N.B., where you can take cars to Port Mulgrave. The all-rail route from Boston to Port Mulgrave is also popular with many.

My favorite route is to take the International morning boat to Portland, ME. The sail is one of the most enjoyable on the eastern coast; the steamers of this line are large and elegant, and the whole voyage is an ever-changing delightful succession of most beautiful seaboard views of Massachusetts, New Hampshire, and a portion of Maine. Arriving at Portland in the afternoon, I spend a few hours in that city, and in the evening take the express train on the Maine Central Railroad. The boat leaves Portland later in the afternoon, and arrives at St. John a little after two o'clock on the afternoon of the next day. The Maine Central and New Brunswick railroads, over which we pass between Portland and St. John, are both well managed and equipped lines, and it is a pleasure to travel over them.

Arriving at St. John, the tourist may spend a day very enjoyably in that queer old city, but it is necessary for him to leave on the 10 p.m. train from St. John in order that he may connect with the steamer at Port Mulgrave, on the afternoon of the next day. The Intercolonial Railway runs through interesting portions of New Brunswick and Nova Scotia, and some of the views to be had from the train in the last named Province are among the finest in eastern America. Leaving the cars at Port Mulgrave and embarking on the steamer, we find ourselves on a neat, comfortable boat, the *Marion*. From Port Mulgrave a good view is obtained of the celebrated Strait of Canso, which is the great highway through which the fishing vessels, steamers and other craft pass to the Gulf of St. Lawrence. After crossing the strait and touching at Port Hawksbury, the steamer passes along the shore of Cape Breton for several hours, giving the tourist a most beautiful panoramic view of lovely bays, headlands, forests and smiling farms. At length the first lock of St. Peter's Canal is entered. This canal, which runs from the Strait of Canso to the Bras D'Or Lake, is a fine specimen of engineering enterprise. Passing into the lake, one may spend a month most delightfully about the shores of this beautiful inland sea.

The most important town on the island is Sydney. Near Sydney are one or two fine rivers—the Myra, twelve miles from the town, being an early salmon stream of considerable importance, as is also the Sydney River. At Baddeck the fisherman who is destined for the Margaree River leaves the steamer and secures a team for his long drive inland. A team chartered and the baggage packed, we start for the village of North East Margaree, our stopping place while we fish. The drive from Baddeck is about twenty-five miles in length. The road winds among and over the mountains, affording superb views of the country for miles on either side. Forests in long stretches and well cultivated farms alternate, and vistas of exceeding beauty open

With a team chartered and the baggage packed, it's off to the fishing grounds.

up on every hand. As the carriage reaches the summit of some towering hill, the almost boundless stretch of forest softening away in the
horizon into a faint blue, broken here and there by the rugged sides
of a towering mountain, makes a scene of beauty and grandeur quite
beyond the power of description.

About half-way between Baddeck and the Margaree is the Middle
River, a famous stream for large sea trout, and salmon are also often
taken in its waters. We reached this river at about midday, and as the

driver informed us that it was the proper thing to stop here, eat
lunch, bait the horses, and cast for trout, we followed his advice,
rigged our tackle and were soon busy casting in the pool below the
big rapids near the road. We soon found that the pool contained a
large number of 'educated trout,' of generous size.

We cast for at least half an hour, and not a rise did we get,
although we could see many large fish moving about in the crystal
depths. Surface fishing was evidently something that they knew all
about. Our flies were very attractive and all that, but they were old
acquaintances, and the trout begged to be excused. The sight of so

many beauties, however, put me on my mettle.

The river swept down over several boulders and a ledge of slate stone, and pitched down sharply into the pool, which was below the rapids fifteen or twenty feet in depth. There was a strong current where the main body of the river swept across the pool, and I thought I saw a chance for outwitting the diffident ones. Putting on my leader a quite large gray hackle, called by most anglers the 'gray mouse,' I dropped it into the water, and letting it sink, permitted the

The James Ross House at North East Margaree ca. 1890s

current to carry it away down almost to the foot of the pool. When the line tautened, at a length of about twenty-five yards, I gave it a few gentle twitches and began to draw it toward me through the rushing waters.

In a moment's time the reel was singing merrily as a three-pounder seized the fly, and such sport as he gave me on my eight-ounce rod for a good five minutes before he came to the landing net! The gray mouse was a revelation to those sea trout, and I picked out enough nice ones for supper in a very short time. When our driver gazed upon them his face wore a thoughtful expression, but he made no comment.

After we and our horses had lunched, we started again on our journey, and at about five o'clock our destination—the village of North East Margaree—came in sight. And what a lovely view it was as we stopped on the brow of the hill. The quiet little village with its trim farm houses and its little church situated in the lovely river intervale, in the midst of well-tilled farms, and the whole surrounded by mountains, which stretched away in ranges as far as the eye could reach.

Our stopping place was to be the house of a Mr. James J. Ross. I am particular to give his full name, for of the thirty-eight or thirty-nine families in this section living up and down the river, thirty-three of them are named Ross, and as he keeps one of the few houses that are fit to stop at, or in which tourists and fishermen are taken, it is important that those who contemplate visiting that region shall know whom to address in order to secure board and rooms. If he cannot take in the new comer there are other houses near by that will, best among which is that kept by the village postmistress; but as Ross

Joseph Revere of Canton, Mass., said to be a grandson of Paul Revere, frequented the Margaree in the early 1900s.

owns the teams and knows all the best pools in the country, and is at all times available as driver, guide, and general utility man, his house is much the best to stop at.

It was a small, unpretentious structure situated in the midst of luxuriant farms. How he and his very good other half managed to pack away in it all the boarders that they had, has always been a mystery to me. He has now, however, an addition built to his old house that is capable of holding comfortably all the guests that are likely to offer.

Here the angler has all the river and brook fishing the most enthusiastic could desire. Immediately back of Ross' house is a brook of considerable size, large enough in many places for good fly-casting. The pools in this brook contain great numbers of fine sea trout and large spotted or brook trout, called by the settlers 'river trout.' These latter fish never descend to the sea, and are as high-colored as any trout I ever saw. I doubt, if they were laid side by side with choice Rangeley specimens, that any one could distinguish them apart. I have seen in the beautiful pool called Solomon's Cellar, many dozens at a time that would weigh from three to six pounds each. These trout, from long familiarity with the usual run of flies, are also 'educated,' and they will only rise at early morn and dewy eve.

Beyond the brook is the beautiful Margaree River, the Plaster Pool being only about half a mile from the house. This river is unique in the Provinces, for it flows for upward of thirty miles through meadows and cultivated farms, and every pool in this long stretch may be reached easily and almost dry-shod.

Below and above the settlement there are some of the finest salmon pools imaginable, at least a dozen being within six miles. In all of these magnificent pools sea trout of great size and gaminess are abundant, and in the right season salmon also; but it is almost useless to fish the river for salmon if the water is low and clear, for the net and spear quickly take out all the fish that have run in, and the fly-fisherman has his labor for his pains. If there is a good fall of rain so as to raise and color the water of the river, thereby rendering spearing impracticable, the fresh run of salmon fills the pools and the fishing is magnificent.

It is a fine river, one of the best in the Dominion, if the spearers and netters would let it alone. I was up the river some twenty or thirty miles from its mouth, and was casting in one of the finest pools I ever saw. At every cast I expected a rise, for the water was right, and the pool looked as if it ought to have at least a dozen fish in it. I worked with the greatest care and patience, and covered the pool in all directions with every variety of fly that I thought ought to move the capricious beauties, but not a rise did I get, except from a few insignificant trout. I could not quite understand it at first, for I knew that the salmon were ascending the river, as they had been taken in a number of the pools below. At length, however, when I went to the foot of the pool and crossed over to the rocks on the other side, I found a number of tell-tale remnants of burned rolls of birch-bark. A roll of blazing birch-bark, and its flame, lights up the water brilliantly wherever the rays of the light penetrate. The fish pay no attention to the blaze, or if they do they are attracted by it, for they seem to swim in the circle of light, but not beyond it. The spearer, standing crouched behind the burning bark, holds his weapon in readiness for a quick thrust and I am told by those who have seen it done, that the blow is given by a practiced hand with the rapidity of lightning.

I returned to my first position at the rapids, at the head, and began casting again but I had no faith in my work, for I knew that the poacher had forestalled me. Presently I was joined by a man who had been at work in the adjacent hay field, and we soon entered in conversation.

"Gitting any fish?" he asked.

"No, nothing but a few sea trout," I replied. "It's strange I don't

Sport Charlie Chandler with river guide Jim Alex Bennett. The arm-chair would suggest that Margaree guides spared no effort in making their clients comfortable.

move a salmon; there ought to be some here, but I haven't stirred a fin yet."

"Yes, it's about time for um to be running up," he answered, naively, "and, in fact, my boys seen some here a day or two back."

"At all events," I replied, "there's none here now, and I may as well go to the pools further up."

"Perhaps you don't fish right, mister," he answered, "or may be your flies ain't just right; you ought to get a salmon in this water, sure." All this quite innocently.

"Well, I cannot say about the way I fish, whether it is right or not," I said, "but the flies are all right, and I have tried every kind I have. It seems to me there must have been spearing going on here lately," I added, looking him in the eye, and at the same time handing him a cigar. "There are certainly quite a number of birch bark embers lying on the rocks yonder."

"Spearing! Oh, no, mister; there ain't no spearing done around here," he exclaimed in a tone that ought to have convinced me. "Why, look, up yonder lives one of the river wardens," and he pointed to a cottage an eighth of a mile from the pool. "Oh, no, we don't have no spearing in this pool, not much. Well, I must be getting to work again," he said, after watching me a short time in my efforts to rise a fish. "Cast away into the eddy, the other side of the rapids, mister, and may be you'll rise a salmon yet; you're fishing all right, and the flies are good ones; fish careful! Oh no, we don't have no spearing in this pool," he ejaculated, as he disappeared in the bushes behind me.

Now, for real genuine finesse your countryman is not to be outdone by a city dweller, and my man in this instance acted his part perfectly; but he was lying to me all through, as I proved inside of ten minutes.

I was casting in the eddy below the rapids, and had hooked a very fine sea trout. Being alone, my friends having left for the pools above, I had considerable difficulty in killing my fish, but was finally assisted by a youngster ten or twelve years of age, who opportunely arrived on the rocks, and taking my net, landed my fish quite skillfully.

"That's a nice trout, mister," he exclaimed, as he laid the fish upon the beach. "How much will he weigh, s'pose?"

I took out my pocket scales, and found that the trout a little over-ran three and a half pounds.

"He isn't quite as big as the one I got yesterday, though," said the lad. "I got him right there in the bend, 'side of that rock." And he pointed into the pool as he spoke.

"How did you get him, my boy?" I asked, quite innocently. "I should think a large fish would be too much for you." And I began casting again, awaiting his reply.

"A Forty-Eight Pounder." Big, but not the biggest. That distinction rests with Percy MacKenzie and his brother from Saint John, N. B., who, in 1927, landed a 52.5-pound, 47-inch-long salmon after a five-hour struggle.

"Oh, I got him just the way I get a good many more. I snared him!"

"Snared him!" I exclaimed. "How under the sun could you snare a trout?"

"Ho! easy enough," he exclaimed. "All you've got to do is to get some wire, and make a slip-noose on it, and drop it down in front of the trout, and then slip it over his head, and pull like mighty, and he's caught; no get away from that, sure."

"And so you noosed him, hey?" I replied.

"No, I snared him," the boy insisted, "and just at dark, yester-day afternoon, I seen a salmon lying there," pointing into the pool near where I stood, "and I struck him with my spear, but he got away."

"Oh, so you have a salmon spear, have you?" I replied, carelessly, still busy casting. "I should think you were not big enough to handle one."

"Oh, mine's a trout spear," he rejoined. "Mine isn't as big as father's, mine's only for trout."

"And so you spear the trout, do you, in addition to snaring them," said I. "Why, you are quite a smart fisherman; it is not every boy of your age who can catch fish the ways you can."

"I guess," he answered, naively.

"And what kind of spear has your father got?"

"Oh, his is a reg'lar salmon spear, and he knows how to use it, too, I can tell you; why the folks around here say he is the boss spearer."

"Is that your father at work there in the meadow yonder?" I asked, pointing to the man who had lately visited me at the pool.

"Yes, that's my father," said the lad. "He's haying."

"And you say he's the champion spearer, is he?" I continued in the same careless tone. "How many salmon do you suppose he can spear in a night if he has good luck? I once knew an Indian that killed five in one night."

"Oh, my pa sometimes gets ten in a night—he's boss." This with a proud tone.

"And what do you do with so many? I should think you would get tired of so much salmon all the time."

"Oh, ma corns (salts) them for winter. Last week, Pa, he speared a big one, the biggest I ever seen in all my life."

"Where did he get him?" I asked.

"Oh, in the pool up there," and he pointed to a pool up the river, in plain view from the warden's house.

"What, in that pool! I should think the spearers would be afraid of the warden."

"Ho! They ain't afraid of him much."

"So!" I exclaimed, carelessly, "what would they do if he came to the pool when they were at work spearing?"

"They'd take rocks and stone him out o' that! He'd be glad to let them alone."

"Ah, did he ever get stoned away?" I asked.

"He did that," was the reply. "Oh, he won't trouble anyone."

"So your father killed the big salmon?" I continued.

"Yes, he was a buster," replied the boy. "You see he laid in this pool two or three days, and all the neighbors tried to get him, but he was too big for any spear they had. He was struck hard more than once, and he had a big gash on his back when father got him. They drove him out of this pool, chasing him so much."

"What do you mean by saying he was too big for any of the spears?" I asked.

"Oh, his back was so thick that the tines wouldn't spread enough. Pa got a spear made all iron, and that fetched him pretty quick. He was a big one!"

"How much did he weigh?" I asked, reeling in my line, and preparing to leave.

While at North East Margaree a pedestrian trip away up the river will be something that the angler and tourist will enjoy. He will need to take an outfit for camping, as he will be gone several days.

"Thirty-eight pounds, and over," was the boy's reply.

"He was a good one," I exclaimed. "Well, I think I'll be going now," I said, gathering up the few trout I had taken.

"There isn't much fun fishing the way you do, mister," said the youngster. "It must be as hard work as chopping wood. A drag-net is the thing to catch a lot of trout with!"

"Yes," I replied, quite embarrassed. "What a lot of big fish I could sweep out of the pool with a good-sized net!"

"Well, not so great many to-day, mister," answered the lad. "The folks over in that house," pointing to a farm house across the river, "have got a large net, big enough to stretch away over the pool, and they catch lots of trout."

"Ah," said I carelessly, "when did they sweep the pool last, my boy?"

"Last night, mister, and they got a pile of big ones! Mister, say, gimme a fly-hook." I handed the youth tribute in the shape of a gray hackle, and went on my way in a meditative mood. As I passed the meadow, I saw the farmer who was still at his work in the hay field, and I almost seemed to hear him muttering to himself, "Spearing! Oh, no, mister, there ain't no spearing done round here, not much!"

I know of no other river that can be fished for such a distance with as little effort from the angler, and the beauty of it all is there are hardly any black flies or mosquitoes to annoy one. Of course, up the river, among the barrens and

Two Margaree beauties.

in the mountains, twenty miles or so, there will be flies, and savage ones, too, but in the open country below through which the river takes its course, no annoyance from the usual pests is experienced.

While at North East Margaree a pedestrian trip away up the river will be something that the angler and tourist will enjoy. He will need to take an outfit for camping, as he will be gone several days. A few miles up the river, at what is called the Middle Section, is one of the most magnificent pools in the Province. Continuing on up the river, the road soon becomes a mere path and before many more miles are passed, the shores of the river become the only thoroughfare to be depended upon. At the Three Forks one pauses for the first camping place and he may here take all the sea trout, and good ones, too, that he can dispose of. In fact the pools are now filled with these delicious fish, with now and then a specimen of the higher colored but less gamey spotted trout. At every cast in the larger pools one is likely to rise a salmon, so that it is better to carry strong tackle along, and not depend on a light single-handed trout rod.

Near this point are the celebrated falls, two hundred feet in height, and beyond these the salmon do not pass. The ascent of the river may be continued for a number of miles further but when you have reached a point where climbing is an effort of the most arduous kind and the river but a noisy rushing mountain stream you will lose your enthusiasm. At Cape Clear, as it is called, you perforce come to a stop, and your ambition will lead you soon to turn about and return to the village.

Mose Murphy, noted Margaree guide, tries his hand at a salmon ca. 1927.

I remember a particularly maddening instance on the Margaree. I was fishing that splendid pool called the Brook Pool about two miles below the settlement at North East Margaree. It is long, deep and wide, and famous for sea trout and salmon. At its head the river flows over steep rapids, and immediately below them a large brook joins it, pouring in a generous supply of cool, clear water; at the junction of the brook and river the pool is very deep, and there is a big eddy two good casts in width, which whirls and swirls about in a lively manner. In this eddy, and on each side and below it, the salmon love to lie, and many an exciting fight have its shores witnessed.

I was fishing the pool early in the morning on the occasion that I refer to, and everything seemed right for a good day's sport; there had been a smart rain on the preceding day, and the water was well colored and running strong. I had made but a few casts when a large sea trout took my fly, and it splashed around considerably before I could land it. It spoiled my fly, and I was obliged to change it. While I was changing my flies, I stepped back upon the beach, and after a new fly was on I stopped to light my pipe, with my back to the pool, when suddenly I heard a loud splash. Turning on the instant, I saw the circles on the water where a heavy fish had evidently just sunk in the middle of the eddy.

"Ah! my beauty," I exclaimed. "I thought you were there; let's try for a better acquaintance."

I waded out again and began casting, and was soon fast to a large fish, which proved to be a four-pound red-spotted brook trout. The current was so strong and the fish so heavy that I could not prevent it from rushing into the best part of the pool, when in a twinkling four salmon jumped into the air almost simultaneously, probably having been stirred up by the casting line striking them as the trout dashed in their midst.

Whew, what a 'kick up' they made. One was a small fish only of about eight pounds weight, two were, I should judge, about twelve pounds each, and the other was an old patriarch of about thirty pounds. Now, there is not another pool in the Dominion that is better than that one to kill a salmon in, and I was just wild to try conclusions with the big one. I landed that trout in the shortest possible time, and putting on a large bright fly on account of the depth and color of the water, I began casting again. I worked, I should think, a good quarter of an hour, but not a rise rewarded my efforts. I then changed for a big showy Silver Doctor that I bought of Scribner, of St. John.

That started the salmon, and such fun as they had with me! Sometimes one would come up, and often two at a time; they leaped all around the fly and over it, and the big one actually jumped into the air after it; they cavorted around there for a long time playing with the fly, but did not offer to take it. This was quite a new experience with me in salmon fishing, although I had seen trout play the same capers.

Well, I held that pool the entire day, changing flies and casting, and resting it, in the vain expectation of getting one of the fish.

Several times during the day did they repeat their morning's performance, and the big one was just as playful as the others; but greatly to my disgust I finally had to abandon the pool and its capricious inhabitants, and go home, 'a sadder yet wiser man.'

One can pass two or three weeks very pleasantly and profitably at North East Margaree. The scenery is charming—in many places picturesque—and it is often grand. Forest-topped and green mountains environ the settlement completely. Lovely vistas of meadows and elm-studded valleys stretch away in all directions. Beautiful drives on good roads are available, and with such fishing as may be had there the time passes delightfully.

When you leave North East Margaree on your return home, I advise, instead of returning to Baddeck by the road over which you came, to drive to Lake Ainslee and thence to Whykokomagh on the Little Bras D'Or and thence by steamer to Baddeck. For the first five or six miles the road follows the windings of the river and I do not remember of anything elsewhere that can compare with the beauty of the views to be had all along. Near the forks of the Margaree, the road to Lake Ainslee branches off from the main road and leads in an easterly direction. It follows the southeast branch of the river and the varied panoramic surprises, which continually meet the eye, arouse to enthusiasm the most indifferent.

About twenty miles from the Ross settlement the road passes the outlet of Lake Ainslee, which forms the head of the southeast branch. Near the head of the lake is a stream which empties into it. Spanning this is a bridge that was, when we crossed it, so dilapidated as to be absolutely unsafe for loaded carriages, and we were obliged to alight and cross it afoot. Below this bridge is a large deep pool, worth a long journey to see. The water is as clear as crystal, from five to twenty feet in depth, and throughout the summer is absolutely packed with sea trout.

As I crossed the bridge I looked down into the water below, and such a sight I never before witnessed. The trout were in thousands, and large ones most of them were, too. This pool is celebrated throughout this portion of the island, and many fine catches have been taken from it. In years past it has been poached badly, and is even now somewhat, but not to the degree that it was a few years ago, a warden now almost constantly supervising it. I am told that in

1884 or 1885 a man 'jigged' out of this pool in one day three barrels of these splendid fish!

We stopped for the night at a farm house hotel near the bridge, kept by a Mr. McLean. Soon after our arrival, haunted by the vision of the host of trout I had seen, I took my rod and sauntered down to the bridge to ascertain whether or not they were interested in entomology. I tried them with various hackles and other flies that I thought would please them but they had been 'educated.' They had seen similar offerings before, and for two hours I succeeded in landing only three or four small fish, evidently unsophisticated new-comers.

Such a sight I never before witnessed. The trout were in thousands, and large ones most of them were, too.

One or two of the neighboring farmers stood on the bridge talking to each other and to me in, I have no doubt, pure Gaelic, the language of most of the Cape Breton 'habitans,' and evidently enjoying 'larks' at my expense in casting over the fish so industriously. Whatever they said, I could not understand a word, the Gaelic tongue not having been mastered by me, so I paid no attention to them. After a while with a parting 'snicker' they left the bridge for their homes, and I was alone.

The sun now hung above the western horizon, a huge red sphere. The skies were covered with the most gorgeous clouds of golden and purple hues, and a soft balmy breeze sprung up. I ceased casting, and, taking a seat on one of the cross beams of the bridge, lighted a cigar and gave myself up to the enjoyment of the magnificent scene before me. The bridge was only a half dozen rods from the lake shore and an unobstructed view could be had for the entire distance to the further shore. Across the bosom of the lake the rays of the setting sun swept in a broad pathway of crimson and gold. The azure of the sky, the gorgeous coloring of the clouds, the green forests and fields of the shore, all were mirrored on the placid water with the most effect. It was a scene to be remembered—entrancing, enrapturing.

I was enjoying it with all the artistic sense of the beautiful in nature that I possessed when I was awakened from my reverie by a heavy splash made by a large fish in the water below me. I looked down, and at that instant another fish came to the surface and with a splash seized a gnat that had dropped upon the water.

"Oh, ho, my beauties! It is a small fly you want, is it? I will try to accommodate you."

Searching among my feathered treasures, I found a small black

gnat, too small, I feared, to be strong enough to bear the strain of a heavy fish. However, I put it on my casting line and dropped it down upon the water, giving it a little flutter at the same time. In an instant my reel was singing merrily as I struck the rise which came instantly, and I was fast to a good two-pound fish.

I was alone and was obliged to land the trout unassisted. It was a difficult operation, for the fish was lively and strong, and I feared for my small hook. I

passed the rod from hand to hand outside the beams of the bridge as I moved along to the beach where I had left my landing net. After I reached it I had to play the fish until it was completely conquered, for I had a small light rod, and this took considerable time. However, after creeling the trout I had a good hour of twilight left, which I improved by taking three more very nice fish, and some smaller ones.

When I showed my catch at the hotel it was pronounced 'very handsome,' but I doubt if any of those who saw it believed I took it with anything but the, in that section, popular jig. In fact I noticed one or two persons examining the bodies of the fish for 'hook marks.'

To an angler the pleasures of the rod and reel are far-reaching, and have no boundary save when the mind ceases to anticipate and the brain to remember. I have had the grandest sport on a midwinter's night with the snow piled high outside and the north wind roaring down the chimney while I sat with my feet to the blaze on the hearth, holding in my hand an old fly-book.

The smoke from my lighted pipe, aided by imagination, contained rod, fish, creel, odorous balsam, drooping hemlock, and purling brook or ruffled lake. I seemed to hear the twittering birds, leaves rustled by the wind, and the music of running water, while the incense of wild flowers saluted my nostrils. The heat of the fire was but the warm rays of the sun, and the crackle of the burning wood the noise of the forest. Thus streams that I have fished once or twice have been fished a score of times.

I had nothing to show for the later fishing, but I could feel that God was good and my memory unimpaired. The fish in the pipe smoke has been as active as was the fish in the water, and afforded as fine play. My reel clicked as merrily, and my rod bent to the play of the fish in the half-dream as they did in the long ago.

Yes there is no recreation that ministers to the poetic in our nature as does the art of angling with the fly-rod, and there is nothing that, to me, gives such pure, innocent and healthful enjoyment. It is over thirty years since I killed my first large fish on the fly. During the period that has elapsed since then, angling has been my chief recreation, yet I have never regretted one moment of the time I have devoted to it. Is there any other pastime that could have given me such unalloyed satisfaction? Assuredly not; and I repeat, there is absolutely nothing that can afford such complete and perfect pleasure as can the fly-rod.

In addition to the pleasure that is derived from the use of the fly-rod, it furnishes the best gymnasium, the best doctor, the best cure for narrow chests, pallid faces, weak nerves, and poor digestions to be found; and if our women wish the enjoyment of perfect health, they should give their attention to angling with the fly.
Edward Samuels, 1890

CHAPTER 9

**ALBERT
BIGELOW
PAINE**
American
sportsman and
author of
The Tent Dwellers,
1905

*Milford House began as
a stage coach stop in the
1860s but within twenty
years was one of the first
hotels, if not the first, in
the province to welcome
non-resident sportsmen.
During the hey-day
of the first two
decades of the
1900s, it catered to
100 sportsmen at a
time; one especially
busy year saw 700
arrive throughout
the season. It is now
into its second centu-
ry of continuous
operation, although
the sport and guests
have changed
markedly since those
times.*

INTO THE DEEP UNKNOWN

*Many and enthusiastic are those sportsmen who assert that South Milford is the
finest holiday ground in all of Nova Scotia. It is situated in Annapolis County at
the headwaters of the Liverpool (Mersey) River, and is a starting point for
excursions into the very heart of the forest. The Milford House offers splendid
accommodation and a colony of cabins surround the main hotel. As a trout region
this is far famed and for moose it is equally renowned. Wonderful canoe routes
radiate in all directions. Down the Liverpool lakes and the Maitland River, past
Maitland to Fairy Lake, one comes again to a perfect maze of alluring side trips.
One is a particular favorite across Fairy Lake and Rossignol, thence to the sea.
Or one may turn from Rossignol to the famous Tobeatic waters. From South
Milford to East Branch there is a carry to Frog, Bear, George and Henry lakes,
thence to the Medway River. From here one may descend to the Atlantic or pene-
trate farther into the interior to Lake Alma. Other trips are to Thomas Meadow,
Frozen Ocean to Fairy Lake and from Flanders Meadows to Bear River. One
may even work over to the Sissiboo or Tusket rivers and come out near
Yarmouth. In all these various trips trout everywhere abound and the moose
roam the country over.*

Morning Chronicle/Evening Echo, 1924

It was possible to put our canoes into one of the lakes near the
[Milford] hotel and enter the wilderness by water–the Liverpool
chain–but it was decided to load boats and baggage into wagons and
drive through the woods–a distance of some seventeen uneven

miles—striking at once for the true wilderness where the larger trout were said to dwell and the "over Sunday" fisherman does not penetrate. Then for a day or two we would follow waters and portages familiar to our guides, after which we would be on the borders of the unknown, prepared to conquer the wilderness.

I shall not soon forget that morning drive to Jake's Landing, at the head of Lake Kedgeemakoogee, where we put in our canoes, a hard, jolting drive over a bad road, with only a break here and there where there is a house or two, and maybe a sawmill and a post-office, the last sentinels of civilization.

It was not much of a place to camp. There was little shade, a good deal of mud, and the sun was burning hot. There was a remnant of black flies, too, and an advance guard of mosquitoes. I was more interested in the loading of the canoes. Del, stout of muscle and figure—not to say fat, at least not over fat—and Charlie, light of weight and heart—sometimes known as Charles the Strong—were packing and fitting our plunder into place, condensing it into a tight and solid compass in the center of our canoes in a way that commanded my respect and even awe. I could see, however, that when our craft was loaded the water line and the gunwale were not so far apart, and I realized that one would want to sit decently still in a craft like that,

Loaded and ready for the true wilderness where the larger trout were said to dwell and the "over-Sunday" fisherman does not penetrate.

especially in rough water.

The wagons had left us now, and we were alone with our canoes and our guides. We dropped out into the lake–Kedgeemakoogee, the lake of the fairies–a broad expanse of black water, dotted with green islands, and billowing white in the afternoon wind, and just as we rounded I felt a sudden tug at the end of my line, which was trailing out behind the canoe.

"Easy now, easy," he [Del] said. "That's a good one–don't hurry him."

But every nerve in me began to tingle, every drop of blood to move. I was eaten with a wild desire to drag my prize into the boat before he could escape. Then all at once it seemed to me that my line must be fast, the pull was so strong and fixed. But looking out behind, Del saw the water break just then–a sort of double flash.

"Good, you've got a pair," he said. "Careful, now, and we'll save 'em both."

To tell the truth I had no hope of saving either, and if I was careful I didn't feel so. When I let the line go out, as I was obliged to, now and then, to keep from breaking it altogether, I had a wild, hopeless feeling that I could never take it up again and that the prize was just that much farther away. Whenever there came a sudden slackening I was sickened with a fear that the fish were gone, and ground the reel handle feverishly.

Everywhere the same clear, black water, and always the trout, the wonderful, wild, abounding Nova Scotia trout.

Albert Bigelow
Paine, 1905

Two 17" Trout on 1 cast
Bear River, N.S.

I brought my catch near the boatside at last, but it is no trifling matter to get two trout into a net when they are strung out on a six-foot leader, with the big trout on the top fly. Reason dictates that the end trout should go in first and at least twice I had him in, when the big fellow at the top gave a kick that landed both outside. It's a mercy I did not lose both, but at last with a lucky hitch they were duly netted, in the canoe, and I was weak and hysterical but triumphant. Never had I taken such fish in the Adirondack or Berkshire streams I had known, and what was more, these were two at a time!

The wind had freshened, the waves were running higher, and with our heavy canoes the six-mile paddle across would be a risky undertaking. We landed and in a little while the tents were white on the shore, Del and Charlie getting them up as if by conjuring. Then once more we were out in the canoes and the curved rod and the taut line and the singing reel dominated every other force under the wide sky. It was not the truest sport, maybe, for the fish were chiefly taken with trolling flies. But to me, then, it did not matter. Suffice it that they were fine and plentiful. That was joy enough, and then such trout— for there are no trout on earth like those one catches himself—such a camp-fire, such a cozy tent, with the guides' tent facing, and the fire between. For us there was no world beyond that circle of light that on one side glinted among boughs of spruce and cedar and maple and birch, and on the other, gleamed out on the black water.

The night was fairly uneventful. Once I imagined I heard something smelling around the camp, and I remember having a sleepy curiosity as to the size and manner of the beast, and whether he meant to eat us and where he would be likely to begin. I may say, too, that I found some difficulty in turning over in my sleeping-bag, and that it did rain. I don't know what hour it was when I was awakened by the soft thudding drops just above my nose, but I remember that I was glad, for there had been fires in the woods, and the streams were said to be low.

It was dull daylight when I awoke. Through the slit in the tent I could see the rain drizzling on the dead camp-fire. There was a nondescript stir in the guides' tent, and presently the head of Charles protruded a little and was withdrawn. Then that of Del appeared and a little later two extraordinary semi-amphibious figures issued—wordless and still rocking a little with sleep—and with that deliberate precision born of long experience, went drabbling after fuel and water that the morning fire might kindle and the morning pot be made to boil.

We were off after breakfast—a breakfast of trout and flapjacks—the latter with maple sirup in the little eating tent. The flapjacks were Del's manufacture, and his manner of tossing the final large one into the air and catching it in the skillet as it fell, compelled admiration.

The lake was fairly smooth and the rain no longer fell. A gray morning—the surface of the water gray, a gray mantle around the more distant of the islands, with here and there sharp rocks rising just above the depths. It was all familiar enough to the guides, but to me it was a new world. Seated in the bow I swung my paddle joyously, and even with our weighty load it seemed that we barely touched the water. One must look out for the rocks, though, for a sharp point plunged through the bottom of a canoe might mean shipwreck. It is six miles across Kedgeemakoogee and during the passage it rained. It was not what might be termed a "prolonged and continuous downpour." The gray veil lifted from the islands. The clouds broke away. The sun came. Ahead of us was a green shore—the other side of Kedgeemakoogee had been reached.

Charlie Munro shows that Del the Stout was not the only Milford guide adept at handling the skillet.

As this was to be rather a long carry, and as more than one trip would be necessary, it was proposed to make a half-way station for luncheon, at a point where a brook cut the trail. But our procession did not move immediately. In the first place one of the canoes appeared to have sprung a leak, and after our six-mile paddle this seemed a proper opportunity to rest and repair damages. Meantime I tried a few casts in the lake, from a slanting rock, and finally slipped in, as was my custom. Then we found that we did not wish to wait until reaching the half-way brook before having at least a bite of sup. It was marshy and weedy where we were and no inviting place to serve food, but we were tolerably wet, and we had paddled a good way. We got out a can of corned beef and a loaf of bread, and stood around in the ooze, and cut off chunks and chewed and gulped and worked them down into place. Then we said we were ready.

It is the etiquette of portage—of Nova Scotia portage, at least—that the fisherman shall carry his own sporting paraphernalia—which is to say, his rods, his gun, if he has one, his fishing basket and his landing net. Also, perhaps, any convenient bag of tackle or apparel when not too great an inconvenience. It is the business of the guides to transport the canoes, the general outfit, and the stores.

Albert Bigelow Paine, 1905

It was interesting to see our guides load up. Charles swung a huge basket on his back and atop of this, other paraphernalia was piled. At the last moment both Charlie and Del stooped and took bundles in each hand. I was really on the very point of offering to carry something, only there was nothing more to carry but the canoes, and of course they had to be left for the next trip. It was well into the afternoon before the canoes reached the end of the carry. It was swampy, and frogs, mosquitoes and midges possessed the locality. We anointed for the mosquitoes and "no-see-ums," as the midges are called by the Indians.

I wonder, by the way, what mosquitoes were made for. I can't think of anything that I could do without easier than the mosquito.

He seems to me a creature wholly devoid of virtues. He is a glutton, a poisoner, a spreader of disease, a dispenser of disturbing music. That last is the hardest to forgive. If he would only be still I could overlook the other things. I wonder if he will take his voice with him into the next world. I should like to know, too, which place he is bound for. I should like to know, so I could take the other road.

Across Mountain Lake was not far, and then followed another short carry—another link of removal—to a larger lake, Pescawess. It was nearly five miles across Pescawess, but we made good time, for there was a fair wind. Also we had the knowledge that Pescawah Brook flows in on the other side, and the trout there were said to be large and not often disturbed. We camped a little below this brook. There were fish. Singly and in pairs they came—great, beautiful, mottled fellows—sometimes leaping clear of the water like a porpoise, to catch the fly before it fell. There were none less than a pound, and many over that weight. When we had enough for supper and breakfast—a dozen, maybe—we put back the others that came, as soon as

taken from the hook. The fishing soon ended then, for I believe the
trout have some means of communication, and one or two trout
returned to a pool will temporarily discourage the others. It did not matter. I had had enough, and once more, returned to the camp, jubilant.

It was raining next morning, but that was not the worst. During
the night I had awakened with a curious, but not entirely unfamiliar
sensation about one of my eyes. There was a slight irritant, itching
tendency, and the flesh felt puffy to the touch. I tried to believe it was
imagination, and went to sleep again. But there was no doubt next
morning. Imagination is a taunting jade, but I don't believe she could
close one of my eyes and fatten up the other—not in so short a time.
It was poison ivy—that was what it was—and I had it bad.

We remained two days in that camp. It rained most of the time, so
the delay did not matter. Indeed it was great luck that we were not
held longer by that distressing disorder which comes of the malignant
three-leaved plant known as mercury, or poison ivy. But the whiskey

treatment was a success. Many times a day I bathed my face in the pure waters of the lake and then with the spirits—rye or Scotch, as happened to be handy. By the afternoon of the first day I could see to put sirup on my flapjacks.

Some kind of alcoholic drink should be taken into the woods. The quantity need not be great and the Puritans need not take it as a beverage even after landing a whopping pair, but I have seen it save the comfort of a party many a time. The guides themselves are in no sense drinking men, but at the close of a hard day, or just after a carry of a mile, they appreciate a wee drappie, and of course, one can't see them do it alone, but the very difficulty of transporting bottles for two or three weeks keeps even the chronically thirsty man temperate. In general whiskey while in the woods is to be condemned. Drunk sparingly and more for the purpose of celebration, it has its place in the quartermaster's department.

Eddie Breck

By the next morning, after a night of sorrow—for my face always pained and itched worse when everybody was in bed and still, with nothing to soothe me but the eternal drip, drip from the boughs and from the eaves of the tent—the swelling was still further reduced, and I felt able to travel. And I wish to add here in all seriousness that whatever may be your scruples against the use of liquors, don't go into the woods without whisky—rye or Scotch, according to preference. Alcohol, of course, is good for poison ivy, but whisky is better. Maybe it is because of the drugs that wicked men are said to put into it. Besides, whisky has other uses. The guides told us of one perfectly rigid person who, when he had discovered that whisky was being included in his camp supplies, had become properly incensed, and commanded that it be left at home. The guides had pleaded that he need not drink any of it, that they would attend to that part of what seemed to them a necessary camp duty, but he was petrified in his morals, and the whisky remained behind. Well, they struck a chilly snap, and it rained. It was none of your little summer landscape rains, either. It was a deadly cold, driving, drenching saturation. Men who had built their houses on the sand, and had no whisky, were in a bad fix. The waves rose and the tents blew down, and the rigid, fossilized person had to be carried across an over-flowed place on the back of a guide, lifting up his voice meanwhile in an effort to convince the Almighty that it was a mistake to let it rain at this particular time, and calling for whisky at every step. It is well to carry one's morals into the woods, but if I had to leave either behind, I should take the whisky.

It was a short carry to Lake Pescawah. Beyond that water we carried again about a quarter of a mile to a lake called Pebbleloggitch— perhaps for the reason that the Indian who picked out the name couldn't find a harder one. From Pebbleloggitch we made our way by a long canal-like stillwater through a land wherein no man—not even an Indian, perhaps—has ever made his home, for it lies through a weird,

Shelburne bog and river. I could not get rid of the idea that we were pioneers in this desolate spot, and so far as sportsmen were concerned, it may be that we were.

lonely marsh—a sort of meadow which no reaper ever harvested, where none but the wild moose ever feeds. We were nearing the edge of the unknown now. One of the guides had been through this stillwater once before, a long time ago. At the end of it, he knew, lay the upper Shelburne River, which was said to flow through a sheet of water called Irving Lake. But where the river entered the lake and where it left it was for us to learn. Already forty miles or more from our starting point, straight into the wilderness, we were isolated from all mankind, and the undiscovered lay directly before.

We got any amount of fly-casting in the Pebbleloggitch Stillwater, but no trout. I kept Del dodging and twice I succeeded in hooking him, though not in a vital spot. I could have done it, however, if he had sat still and given me a fair chance. I could land Del even with the treetop cast, but the trout refused to be allured. As a rule, trout would not care to live in a place like that. There would not be enough excitement and activity. A trout prefers a place where the water is busy—where the very effort of keeping from being smashed and battered against the rocks insures a good circulation and a constitution like a steel spring. I have taken trout out of water that would have pulverized a golf ball in five minutes. The fiercer the current, the greater the tumult, the more cruel and savage the rocks, the better place it is for trout.

Neither do I remember that we took anything in the Shelburne above Irving Lake, for it was a good deal like the Stillwater, with only a gentle riffle here and there. Besides, the day had become chill, and a mist had fallen upon this lonely world—a wet, white, drifting mist that was closely akin to rain. On such a day one does not expect trout to rise, and is seldom disappointed. As it was, we paddled rather silently down the still river, considerably impressed with the thought that we were entering a land to us unknown—that for far and far in every direction, beyond the white mist that shut us in and half-obliterated the world, it was likely that there was no human soul that was not of our party and we were quieted by the silence and loneliness on every hand. I was filled, somehow, with the feeling that must have come over those old Canadian voyageurs who were first to make their way through the northlands, threading the network of unknown waters. I could not get rid of the idea that we were pioneers in this desolate spot, and so far as sportsmen were concerned, it may be that we were.

We paddled a little distance and some islands came out of the gray veil ahead—green Nova Scotia islands, with their ledges of rock, some underbrush and a few sentinel pines. We ran in close to these, our guides looking for moose or signs of them. I may say here that no expedition in Nova Scotia is a success without having seen at least one moose. Of course, in the hunting season, the moose is the prime object, but such is the passion for this animal among Nova Scotia guides, that whatever the season or the purpose of the expedition, and however triumphant its result, it is accounted a disappointment and a failure by the natives when it ends without at least a glimpse of a moose.

We were in wonderful moose country now; the uninvaded wild, where in trackless bog and swamp, or on the lonely and forgotten islands the she-moose secludes herself to bear and rear her young. That Charlie and Del were more absorbed in the possibility of getting a sight of these great, timid, vanishing visions of animal life—and perhaps a longer view of a little black, bleating calf—than in any exploration for the other end of the Shelburne River was evident. They clung and hovered about those islands, poking the canoes into every nook and corner, speaking in whispers, and sitting up straight at sight of any dark-looking stump or bunch of leaves. It was just the sort of a day to see moose, Del said, and there was no other matter that would stand in importance against a proposition like that. I became interested myself, presently, and dropped my voice to a whisper and sat up at every black spot among the leaves. We had just about given it up at length, when all at once Del gave the canoe a great shove inshore, but not too late, for beyond a wide neck of water, on the mainland, two dark phantoms drifted a little way through the mist and vanished into the dark foliage behind.

We now got down to business. It was well along towards evening, and though these days were long days, this one, with its somber skies and heavy mist, would close in early. We felt that it was desirable to find the lake's outlet before pitching our tents, for the islands make rather poor camping places and lake fishing is apt to be slow work. We wanted to get settled in camp on the lower Shelburne before night and be ready for the next day's sport. Then came a diversion. Real rain—the usual night downpour—set in, and there was a scramble to get the tents up and our goods under cover.

As usual, the clouds had emptied themselves by morning. The sky was still dull and threatening, and from the tent door the water of the lake was gray. But the mist had gone, and the islands came out green and beautiful. The conditions made it possible to get some clothing decently smoked and scorched, which is the nearest approach to dryness one is ever likely to achieve in the woods in a rainy season.

I may say here that the time will come—and all too soon, in a period of rain—when you will reach your last dry suit of underwear—and get it wet. Then have a care. Be content to stay in a safe, dry spot, if you can find one—you will have to go to bed, of course, to do it—until something is dry—that is, pretty dry. To change from one wet suit to another only a little less so is conducive neither to comfort nor to a peaceful old age. Above all, do not put on your night garment, or garments, for underwear, for they will get wet, too; then your condition will be desperate.

Kedge guide, Tom Canning, eating lunch at Irving Dam while a pair of wet socks are 'smoked and scorched' over a trail fire.

I submit the above as good advice. I know it is good advice for I did not follow it. I have never followed good advice—I have only given it. At the end of several nights of rain and moist days, I had nothing really dry but my night-shirt and one slipper. What we did was to pick out the least damp of our things and smoke and scorch them on a pole over the camp-fire until they had a sort of a half-done look, like bread toasted over a gas jet; then suddenly we would seize them and put them on hot and go around steaming, and smelling of leaf smoke and burnt dry goods— these odors blended with the fragrance of camphor, tar and penny-royal, with which we were presently saturated in every pore. For though it was said to be too late for blackflies and too early for mosquitoes, the rear guard of the one and the advance guard of the other combined to furnish us with a good deal of special occupation. The most devoted follower of the Prophet never anointed himself oftener than we did, and of course this continuous oily application made it impossible to wash very perfectly; besides, it seemed a waste to wash off the precious protection when to do so meant only another immediate and more thorough treatment.

Fishing and camping, though fairly clean recreations, will be found not altogether free from soiling and grimy tendencies, and when one does not or cannot thoroughly remove the evidences several times a day, they begin to tell on his general appearance. Gradually our hands lost everything original except their shape. Then I found that to shave took off a good deal of valuable ointment each time. Of

course we never gave up the habit altogether; it would break out spo-radically. Washing is a good deal a question of pride, anyway, and pride did not count any more. Even self-respect had lost its charm.

In the matter of clothing, however, I wish to record that I never did put on my nightdress for an undergarment. I was tempted to do so, daily, but down within me a still small voice urged the rashness of such a deed and each night I was thankful for that caution. If one's things are well smoked and scorched and scald-ed and put on hot in the morning, he can forget presently that they are not also dry, and there is a chance that they may become so before night; but to face the prospect of getting into a wet garment to sleep, that would have a tendency to destroy the rare charm and flavor of camp life. In time I clung to my dry nightshirt as to a life-belt. As for the guides, I have a notion that they prefer wet clothes.

There were quantities of trout in the lower Shelburne, and in a pool just below the camp, next morning, [we] took a dozen or more—enough for breakfast and to spare—in a very few minutes. They were lively fish—rather light in color, but beautifully marked and small enough to be sweet and tender, that is, not much over a half-pound weight. In fact, by this time we were beginning to have a weakness for the smaller fish. The pound-and-upward trout, the most plentiful size, thus far, were likely to be rather dry and none too tender. When we needed a food supply, the under-sized fish were more welcome, and when, as happened only too rarely, we took one of the old-fash-ioned New England "speckled beauty" dimensions—that is to say, a trout of from seven to nine inches long and of a few ounces weight—it was welcomed with real joy. Big fish are a satisfaction at the end of a line and in the landing net, but when one really enters upon a trout diet—when at last it becomes necessary to serve them in six or seven different ways to make them go down—the demand for the smallest fish obtainable is pretty certain to develop, while the big ones are promptly returned with good wishes and God-speed to their native element. For of course no true sportsman ever keeps any trout he cannot use. Only the "fish-hog" does that.

In spite of the rains the waters of the Shelburne were too low at this point to descend in the canoes. The pools were pretty small affairs and the rapids long, shallow and very ragged. It is good sport to run rapids in a canoe when there is plenty of swift water and a fair percentage of danger. But these were dangerous only to the canoes, which in many places would not even float, loaded as we were. It became evident that the guides would have to wade and drag, with here and there a carry, to get the boats down to deeper water—provided always there was deeper water, which we did not doubt.

[We] set out ahead, and having had our morning's fishing, kept pretty well to the bank where the walking was fairly

There are, I fancy, few places where a disciple of the "gentle Isaac" can more readily and successfully indulge in his favorite pastime of trout fishing than in Nova Scotia.

Frederick Harris D. Vieth, 1907

good. We felt pleasant and comfortable and paid not much attention to the stream, except where a tempting pool invited a cast or two, usually with prompt returns, though we kept only a few, smaller fish. We found the banks more attractive. Men had seldom disturbed the life there, and birds sang an arm's length away, or regarded us quietly, without distrust. Here and there a hermit thrush—the sweetest and shyest of birds—himself unseen, charmed us with his mellow syllables. Somehow, in the far, unfretted removal of it all, we felt at peace with every living thing.

It was about one o'clock when we reached a really beautiful stretch of water, wide and deep, and navigable for an indefinite distance. Here we stopped to get fish for luncheon, and to wait for the boats, which we anticipated at any moment. It was a wonderful place to fish. One could wade out and get long casts up and down, and the trout rose to almost any fly. The place seemed really inexhaustible. I think there were few trout larger than fourteen inches in length, but of these there were a great many, and a good supply of the "speckled beauty" size. When we had enough of these for any possible luncheon demand, and were fairly weary of casting and reeling in, we suddenly realized that we were hungry; also that it was well into the afternoon and that there were no canoes in sight. It began to be necessary that we should have a camp and be fed. Still we waited hopefully, expecting every moment to see the canoes push around the bend.

Eventually we were seized with misgivings. It was well toward night when we began to realize the positive necessity of locating our guides and canoes. We had given up trying to understand the delay. We decided to follow back up the river until we found them, or until we reached some other branch which they might have chosen. It was just as we were about to begin this discouraging undertaking that far up the bend we heard a call, then another. We answered, both together, and in the

We hurried back to meet two of the weariest, wettest, most bedraggled mortals that ever poled and dragged and carried canoe.

reply we recognized the tones of Charles the Strong. Presently they came in sight—each dragging a canoe over the last riffle just above the long hole. A moment later we had hurried back to meet two of the weariest, wettest, most bedraggled mortals that ever poled and dragged and carried canoe. All day they had been pulling and lifting; loading, unloading and carrying those canoes and bags and baskets over the Shelburne riffles, where not even the lightest craft could float. How long had been the distance they did not know, but the miles had been sore, tedious miles, and they had eaten nothing more than a biscuit, expecting at every bend to find us waiting.

It was proper that we should make camp now at the first inviting place. We offered to stop right there, where our fire was already going, but it was decided that the ground was a poor selection, being rather low. We piled into the canoes and shot down the long hole, while the light of evening was fading from the sky. Several hundred yards below, the water widened and the bank sloped higher. We decided to camp there and to stay until we were fully repaired for travel. No camp was ever more warmly welcomed, or ever will be more fondly remembered by us all.

The tent, with its daily and nightly round, becomes a rather important thing when it is to be a habitation for a period of weeks of

The tent, with its daily and nightly round, becomes a

rather important thing when it is to be a habitation for a period of weeks of sun and storm.

sun and storm. There is the matter of getting along without friction, which seems important. A tent is a small place, and it is likely to contain a good many things— especially in bad weather—besides yourselves. If you can manage to have your things so the other fellow will stumble over them as infrequently as possible, it is just as well for him, and safer for you. Also, for the things. Then, too, if you will make your beds at separate times, as we did, one remaining outside, or lying in a horizontal position among his own supplies while the other is in active operation, you are less likely to rub against each other, which sometimes means to rub in the wrong direction, with unhappy results. Of course forbearance is not a bad asset to have along, and a small measure of charity and consideration. It is well to take one's sense of humor, too, and any little remnant of imagination one may have lying about handy at the moment of starting. Many a well-constructed camp has gone to wreck during a spell of bad weather because one or more of its occupants did not bring along imagination and a sense of humor, or failed to produce these articles at the critical moment. Imagination beautifies many a desolate outlook—a laugh helps over many a hard place.

We established a good camp on the Shelburne and remained in it for several days. For one thing, our canoes needed a general over-hauling after that hard day on the rocks. Also, it rained nightly, and now and then took a turn at it during the day, to keep in practice. We minded the rain, of course, as it kept us forever cooking our clothes, and restrained a good deal of activity about the camp. Still, we argued that it was a good thing, for there was no telling what sort of water lay ahead and a series of rock-strewn rapids with low water might mean trouble.

On the whole, we were willing to stay and put up with a good deal for the sport in that long pool. There may be better fishing on earth than in the Shelburne River between Irving and Sand lakes, but it will take something more than mere fisherman's gossip to convince me of that possibility. We left the guides and went together one morning, and in less than three hours had taken fully fifty fish of a pound each, average weight. We took off our top flies presently and

fished with only one, which kept us busy enough, and always one of us had a taut line and a curved rod, often both at one time. There was a general rising to anything we offered—Doctors, Parmcheenie, Absorbent Cotton—any old thing that skimmed the water and looked big and succulent.

We broke camp that morn-ing and dropped down toward the next lake—Sand Lake, it would be, by our crude map and hazy directions. There are no better rapids and there is no more lively fishing than we had on that run. There was enough water for us to remain in the canoes, and it was for the most part whirling, swirling, dashing, leaping water—shooting between great boulders, plunging among cruel-looking black rocks—foaming into whirlpools below, that looked ready to swamp our light craft, with

stores, crew, tackle, everything. It was my first exhibition of our guides' skill in handling their canoes. How they managed to just evade a sharp point of rock on one side and by a quick twist escape ship-wreck from a boulder or mass of boulders on the other, I fail to comprehend. Then there were narrow boiling channels, so full of obstructions that I did not believe a chip could go through with entire safety. Yet somehow Del the Stout and Charles the Strong seemed to know, though they had never traveled this water before, just where the water would let the boats pass, just where the stones were wide enough to let us through—touching on both sides, sometimes, and ominously scraping on the bottom, but sliding and teetering into the cauldron below, where somehow we did not perish, perhaps because we shot so quickly through the foam. I presently gave myself up to the pure enjoyment of the tumult and exhilaration, without disturb- ing myself as to dangers here or hereafter.

I do not believe the times that the guides got out of the canoes to ease them over hard places would exceed twice, and not oftener than that were we called on to assist them with the paddles. Even when we wished to do so, we were often requested to go on fishing, for the reason, I suppose, that in such a place one's unskilled efforts are like- ly to be misdirected with fatal results. We went on fishing. I don't know how many fish I took that day, but Eddie kept count of his, and recorded a total of seventy-four between camp and the great, splendid pool where the Shelburne foams out into Sand Lake, four miles or such a matter, below. Of fish we kept possibly a dozen, the smallest ones. The others—larger and wiser now—are still frolicking in the waters of the Shelburne, unless some fish-hog has found his way to that fine water, which I think doubtful, for a fish-hog is usually too lazy and too stingy to spend the effort and time and money necessary to get there.

We looked for moose again on Sand Lake but found only signs. Below Sand Lake a brook was said to enter. Descending from the upper interior country, it would lead us back into regions more remote than any heretofore traveled. So far as I could learn, neither of our guides had ever met anyone who even claimed to know this region, always excepting [an] imaginative Indian. Somewhere in these unchartered wilds this Indian person had taken trout "the size of one's leg." Regardless of the dimensions of this story, it had a fascination for us. We wished to see those trout, even if they had been overrated. We had been hurrying, at least in spirit, to reach the little water gateway that opened to a deeper unknown where lay a chain of lakes, vaguely set down on our map as the Tobeatic waters. At some time in the past the region had been lumbered, but most of the men who cut the timber were probably dead now, leaving only a little drift of heresay testimony behind.

It was not easy to find the entrance to the hidden land. The foliage was heavy and close along the swampy shore, and from such an ambush a still small current might flow unnoticed, especially in the mist that hung about us. More than once we were deceived by some fancied ripple or the configuration of the shore. Del at length announced that just ahead was a growth of a kind of maple likely to indicate a brook entrance. The shore really divided there and a sandy waterway led back somewhere into a mystery of vines and trees.

We halted near the mouth of the little stream for lunch and consultation. It was not a desirable place to camp. The ground was low and oozy and full of large-leaved greenhousy-looking plants. The recent rains had not improved the character of the place. There was poison ivy there, too, and a delegation of mosquitoes. So we stopped and sat around in the mud, and looked at some marks on a paper— made by the imaginative Indian, I think—and speculated as to whether it would be possible to push and drag the canoes up the brook, or whether everything would have to go overland. Personally, the prospect of either did not fill me with enthusiasm. The size of the brook did not promise much in the way of important waters above or fish even the size of one's arm. However, Tobeatic exploration was down on the cards. Our trip thus far had furnished only a hint of such mystery and sport as was supposed to lie concealed somewhere beyond the green, from which only this little brooklet crept out to whisper the secret.

We proceeded up the stream, the guides pushing the loaded canoes behind. It was the brook of our forefathers—such a stream as might flow through the valley meadows of New England, with trout of about the New England size, and plentiful. Lively fellows, from seven to nine inches in length, rose two and three at almost every cast. We put on small flies and light leaders and forgot there were such things as big trout in Nova Scotia. It was joyous, old-fashioned fishing—a real treat for a change.

We had not much idea how far we were to climb this water stairway, and as the climb became steeper, and the water more swift, the guides pushed and puffed and we gave them a lift over the hard places. Then suddenly everything was forgotten, for a gate of light opened out ahead, and presently we pushed through and had reached the shores of as lovely a sheet of water as lies in the great north woods. It was Tupper Lake, by our calculation, and it was on the opposite side that Tobeatic Brook was said to enter. There, if anywhere, we might expect to find the traditional trout. So far as we knew, no one had looked on these waters since the old lumbering days. Except for exploration there was no reason why anyone should come. Of fish and game there were plenty in localities more accessible. To me, I

Kedge guide, Arthur Canning, Wildcat Brook. "Many a time has my canoeman, without a word from me, glanced up to the noonday sun, pulled silently ashore, and lighted the fire for 'b'iling

the kittle.' A pint dipper of strong tea with a biscuit or two has, in a hurried journey, proved sufficient, if followed by the inevitable pipe; and the paddle or setting pole was resumed with renewed vigor."

Edward Samuels, 1890

believe the greatest joy there, as everywhere in the wilderness—and it was a joy that did not grow old—was the feeling that we were in a region so far removed from clanging bells and grinding wheels and all the useful, ugly attributes of mankind.

We put out across the lake. The land rose rather sharply beyond, and from among the trees there tumbled out a white foaming torrent that made a wide swirling green pool where it entered. We had on our big flies now and our heavy leaders. They were necessary. Scarcely had a cast gone sailing out over the twisting water when a big black and gold shape leaped into the air. A moment later my reel was singing, and I knew by the power and savage rushes that I had something unusual at the other end.

"Trout as big as your leg!" we called across to each other, and if they were not really as big as that, they were, at all events, bigger

"Trout as big as your leg!"

than anything so far taken—as big as one's arm perhaps—one's forearm, at least, from the hollow of the elbow to the finger-tips. You see how impossible it is to tell the truth about a trout the first time. I never knew a fisherman who could do it. There is something about a fish that does not affiliate with fact.

We considered the imaginative Indian justified, and blessed him. We took seventeen of those big fellows before we landed, enough in all conscience. A point just back of the water looked inviting as a place to pitch the tents, and we decided to land, for we were tired.

By this time we had reached trout diet *per se*. I don't know what *per se* means, but I have often seen it used and it seems to fit this case. Of course we were not entirely out of other things. We had flour for flapjacks, some cornmeal for mush and Johnnie-cake, and enough bacon to impart flavor to the fish. Also, we were not wholly without beans—long may they wave—the woods without them would be a wilderness indeed. But in the matter of meat diet it was trout *per se,* as I have said, unless that means we did not always have them; in which case I will discard those words. We did. We had fried trout, broiled trout, boiled trout, baked trout, trout on a stick, and trout chowder. We may have had them other ways—I don't remember. I know I began to imagine that I was sprouting fins and gills, and daily I felt for the new bumps on my head, which I was certain must result from this continuous absorption of brain food.

In fact, provisioning for a camping trip is a serious matter. Where a canoe must carry a man and guide, with traps and paraphernalia, and provisions for a three-weeks' trip, the problem of condensation in

Provisioning for a camping trip is a serious matter.... No two canoes can safely carry enough canned beans to last two fishermen and two Nova Scotia guides for three weeks.

the matter of space and weight, with amplitude in the matter of quantity, affords study for a careful mind. We started out with a lot of can and bottle goods, which means a good deal of water and glass and tin, all of which are heavy and take up room. I don't think ours was the best way. The things were good—too good to last—but dried fruits—apricots, prunes and the like—would have been nearly as good, and less burdensome. Indeed by the end of the second week I would have given five cents apiece for a few dried prunes, while even dried apples, which I had learned to hate in childhood, proved a gaudy luxury. Canned beans, too, I consider a mistake. You can't take enough of them in that form. No two canoes can safely carry enough canned beans to last two fishermen and two Nova Scotia guides for three weeks.

As I have said, dried things are better: fruits, beans, rice, beef, bacon, maple sugar (for sirup), cornmeal and prepared flour. If you want to start with a few extras in the way of canned stuff, do it, but be sure you have plenty of the staples mentioned. You will have enough water and tin and glass to carry with your condensed milk, your vinegar, a few pickles, and such other bottle refreshments as your tastes and morals will permit. Take all the variety you can in the way of dried staples—be sure they are staples— but cut close on your bulky tinned supplies. It is better to be sure of enough Johnnie-cake and bacon and beans during the last week out than to feast on plum-pudding and California pears the first.

I would gladly have lingered at Tobeatic

The dying embers of a still smouldering camp-fire are quickly knocked together and fresh fuel is added. From a pothook stretched from a bar supported on a couple of notched stakes, a little tin kettle gives out the grateful fragrance of steaming tea. A cup or two is quaffed, a pipe follows: then blissful sleep such as is not to be had elsewhere than on a bed of 'sapin' or fragrant fir boughs amid the pine-scented forests....

Arthur Silver, 1907

Dam. It was an ideal place, wholly remote from everything human—a haunt of wonderful trout, peaceable porcupines and tame birds. I wanted to rest there, and to heal up a little before resuming the unknown way. But there were more worlds to conquer. Lower Tobeatic Lake was but a little way above. We pushed through to it without much delay. It was an extensive piece of water, full of islands, lonely rocks and calling gulls, who come to this inland isolation to rear their young.

I do not know what lies above the Tobeatic lakes, but the strip of country between is the true wilderness. It is a succession of swamps and spruce thickets—ideal country for a moose farm or a mosquito hatchery, or for general exploration, but no sort of a place for a Sunday-school picnic. Neither is it a good place to fish. The little brook between the lakes runs along like a chain pump and contains about as many trout. There are one or two pretty good pools, but the effort to reach them is too costly.

We made camp in as dry a place as we could find, but we couldn't find a place as big as the tent that didn't have a spring or a water hole. In fact, the ground was a mass of roots, great and small, with water everywhere between. A spring actually bubbled up between our beds, and when one went outside at night it was a mercy if he did not go plunging into some sort of a cold, wet surprise, with disastrous and profane results. Being the worst camp and the worst country and the poorest fishing we had found, we remained there two days. The matter of mosquitoes was really serious that night. We kept up several smudge fires and sat among them and smoked ourselves like herring. Even then we were not immune. When it came time for bed we brushed the inside of the tent and set our pipes going. It was by no means an unpleasant camp, first and last. It was our "Farthest North" for one thing, our deepest point in the wilderness. It would require as much as three or four days' travel, even by the quickest and most direct route, to reach any human habitation, and in this thought there was charm.

Back across Tupper Lake and down Sand Brook to the Shelburne. A distance—I have forgotten the number of miles—down the Shelburne would bring us to country known to the guides. It was beautiful going, down Sand Brook. There was plenty of water and the day was perfect. There is nothing lovelier in the world than that little limpid stream with its pebbly riffles and its sunlit pools. Sometimes when I think of it now I am afraid that it is no longer there in that far still Arcady, or that it may vanish through some enchantment before I can ever reach it again. Indeed as I am writing here to-day I am wondering if it is really there—hidden away in that quiet unvisited place, when no one is there to see it, and to hear it sing and whisper—if anything is anywhere, unless someone is there to see and hear.

I have already said that there is no better trout fishing than in the Shelburne. The fish now were not quite so heavy as they had been higher up, but they were very many. When we were a little above

Kempton Dam, Del pointed out the first place familiar to him. The woods were precisely the same, the waters just as fair and fruitful, the locality just as wild; but somehow as we rounded that bend a certain breath of charm vanished. The spell of perfect isolation was gone. I had the feeling that we had emerged from the enchanted borders of No Man's Land, that we were entering a land of real places, with the haunts and habitations of men. We decided to drop down the river to Lake Rossignol and cross over to the mouth of the Liverpool. It was a long six-mile ferriage across Rossignol.

The Shelburne is rough below Kempton Dam. It goes tearing and foaming in and out among the black rocks, and there are places where you have to get out of the canoes and climb over, and the rocks are slippery and sometimes there is not much to catch hold of. We shot out into the lake at last, and I was glad. It was a mistake, however, to be glad just then. It was too soon. The wind had kicked up a good deal of water, and though our canoes were lighter than when we started, I did not consider them suited to such a sea. They pitched about and leaped up into the air, one minute with the bow entirely out of the water, and the next with it half-buried in the billow ahead. Every other second a big wave ran on a level with the gun-wale, and crested its neck and looked over and hissed, and sometimes it spilled in upon us. It would not take much of that kind of freight to make a cargo, and anything like an accident in that wide, gray billowy place was not a nice thing to contemplate. A loaded canoe would go down like a bullet. No one clad as we were could swim more than a boat's length in that sea.

As we got farther off shore the waves got worse. If somebody had just suggested it I should have been willing to turn around and make back for the Shelburne. Nobody suggested it, and we went on. It seemed to me those far, dim shores through the mist, five miles or more away, would never get any closer. I grew tired, too, and my arms ached, but I could not stop paddling. I was filled with the idea that if I ever stopped that eternal dabbling at the water, my end of the canoe would never ride the next billow. Del reflected aloud, now and then, that we had made a mistake to come out on such a day. When at last we entered the mouth of the Liverpool, we camped there.

There are always compensations for those who suffer and are meek in spirit. That was the evening I caught the big fish. It was just below a big fall—Loon Lake Falls I think they call it—and we were going to camp there. Something that looked big and important, far down the swift racing current, rose to what I had intended as my last cast. I had the little four-ounce bamboo, but I let the flies go down there—the fly, I mean, for I was casting with one (a big Silver Doctor)—and the King was there, waiting. He took it with a great slop and carried out a long stretch of line. It was a test for the little rod. There had been unkind remarks about the tiny bamboo whip;

this was to be justification; a big trout on a long line, in deep, swift water—the combination was perfect.

I shall not dwell upon the details of that contest. I may say, however, that I have never seen Del more excited than during the minutes—few or many, I do not know how few or how many—that it lasted. Every guide wants his canoe to beat, and it was evident from the first that this was the trout of the expedition. I know that Del believed I would never bring that fish to the canoe, and when those heavy rushes came I was harrassed with doubts myself. Then little by little he yielded. When at last he was over in the slower water—out of the main channel—I began to have faith. So he came in, slowly, slowly, and as he was drawn nearer to the boat, Del seized the net to be ready for him. I brought him to the very side of the boat, and I lifted him in. This time the big fish did not get away. We went to where the others had been watching, and I stepped out and tossed him carelessly on the ground, as if it were but an everyday occurrence. I think I shall not give the weight of that fish. As already stated, no one can tell the truth concerning a big fish.

Through the Eel-weir—a long and fruitful rapid—we entered our old first lake, Kedgeemakoogee, this time from another point. We had made an irregular loop of one hundred and fifty miles or more—a loop that had extended far into the remoter wilderness, and had been marked by what, to me, were hard ventures and vicissitudes, but which, viewed in the concrete, was recorded in my soul as a link of pure happiness. We camped that night at Jim Charles' Point, our old first camp, and it was like getting home after long absence. For the time seemed an age since we had left there. It was that. Any new and wonderful experience is long—as long as eternity—whether it be a day or a decade in duration.

Perhaps the brightest spot of that sad period when we were making ready to leave the woods, with all their comfort, their peace and their religion, and go back to the harrying haunts of men, to mingle with the fever and fret of daily strife, is the memory of a trip to Jeremy's Bay. I don't know in the least where Jeremy's Bay is, but it is somewhere within an hour's paddle of Jim Charles' Point, and it is that hour and the return that sticks with me now.

It was among the last days of June—the most wonderful season in the north woods. The sun seems never ready to set there, then, and

Civilization—the world, flesh and the devil— mankind and all the duties of life were as nothing. Here were the woods and the waters. There was the point for the campfire and the tents. About us were the leaping trout. The spell of the forest and the chase gripped me body and soul. Only these things were worth while. Nothing else mattered—nothing else existed.

Albert Bigelow
Paine, 1905

all the world is made of blues and greens and the long, lingering tones of evening. We had early tea in preparation for the sunset fishing. It was best, Del said, in Jeremy's Bay about that time. So it was perhaps an hour earlier when we started, the canoes light.

In any one life there are not many evenings such as that. It is just as well, for I should account it a permanent sadness if they became

monotonous. Perhaps they never would. Our course lay between shores—an island on the one hand, the mainland on the other. When we rounded the point, we were met by a breeze blown straight from the sunset—a breath that was wild and fresh and sweet, and billowed the water till it caught every hue and shimmering iridescence that the sky and shores and setting sun could give. We were eager and rested, for we had done little that day, and the empty canoes slipped like magic into a magical sea of amethyst and emerald gold, the fresh breeze filling us with life and ecstasy until we seemed almost to fly. The eyes could not look easily into the glory ahead, though it was less easy to look away from the enchantment which lay under the sunset. The Kingdom of Ponemah was there, and it was as if we were following Hiawatha to that fair and eternal hunting-ground.

Yet when one did turn, the transformation was almost worth while. The colors were all changed. They were more peaceful, more like reality, less like a harbor of dreams and visions too fair for the eyes of man to look upon. A single glance backward, and then away once more between walls of green, billowing into the sunset—away, away to Jeremy's Bay! The sun was just on the horizon when we reached there—the water already in shadow near the shore. So deep and vivid were its hues that we seemed to be fishing in dyestuff.

And the breeze went out with the sun, and the painted pool became still, ruffled only where the trout broke water or a bird dipped down to drink.

I will not speak of the fishing there. But Jeremy's Bay is a spot that few guides know and few fishermen find. It was our last real fishing, and it was worthy. Then home to camp, between walls of dusk—way, away from Jeremy's Bay—silently slipping under darkening shores—silently, and a little sadly, for our long Day of Joy was closing in; the hour of return drew near. And postpone it as you will, the final moment must come—the time when the rod must be taken down for good, the leaders stripped and coiled in their box, the fly-book tenderly gone over and the last flies you have used fitted into place and laid away.

One does not go through that final ritual without a little sentiment—a little tugging about the heart. The flies were all new and trim and properly placed when you set out. They were a gay array and you were as proud of them as of a little garden. They are in disarray now. They have an unkempt look. The snells are shredded, the feathers are caked and bitten, the hackle is frazzled and frayed out. For a hundred years, if I live that long, this crumpled book and these broken, worn-out flies will bring back the clear, wild water and the green shores of a Nova Scotia June, the remoter silences of the deeper forest, the bright camps by twisting pools and tumbling falls, the flash of the leaping trout, the feel of the curved rod and the music of the singing reel.

When the wind beats up and down the park, and the trees are bending and cracking with ice, when I know that once more the still places of the North are white and the waters fettered, I shall shut my eyes and see again the ripple and the toss of June, and hear once more the under voices of the falls. And some day I shall return to those far shores, for it is a place to find one's soul.

Blessing on the Woods

Blest be our woods of hemlock, maple, pine,
Balsam and birch, dear Lord, our woods and Thine!
Blest be their bubbling springs, their rippling lakes,
Their ponds, and every laughing brook that makes
Rainbows and foam and crystal homes for trout.
Blest be the trails that wander in and out
Among grey boulders drowned in soft green seas
Of velvet Moss! Oh, blest be all of these!

Blest be the woods and they that dwell therein:
The scolding squirrel and his gentler kin,
The friendly chipmunk and the timid hare;
Blest be the graceful mink, the shambling bear,
The beaver on his dam, the drumming grouse,
The hawk that loves the sky, the white-foot mouse,
The antlered buck that paces proud and tall
With doe and dappled fawn, blest be them all!

Lord bless the woods for perfect loveliness,
For balm that heals the soul in care and stress!
Keep them forever fragrant, cool and sweet!
From thunderbolt and flame, from gale and sleet.
From avalanche, from torrent, drought and blight
From all that is unclean, from ruthless might
That gives desolation to valley, glen
And mountainside, God bless our woods! Amen.

Arthur Guiterman

SOURCES

CHAPTER 1   Hardy, Campbell. *Sporting Adventures in the New World.* 2
vols. London: Hurst & Blackett, 1855.

CHAPTER 2   Cobb, Irvin S. *Some United States: A Series of Stops in Various
Parts of This Nation With One Excursion Across the Line.* New
York: George H. Doran Co., 1926.

CHAPTER 3   Breck, Mary. *Outdoor Recreation.* Chicago: Outers' Book
Co., March 1925.

CHAPTER 4   Hardy, Campbell. *Sporting Adventures.* 1855.

CHAPTER 5   Tricoche, G. N. *Rambles Through the Maritime Provinces of
Canada.* London: Arthur H. Stockwell Ltd.
Breck, Edward. "Climbing the Caribou." *Outing.* vol. 63., January 1914.

CHAPTER 6   Silver, Arthur P. *Farm-Cottage, Camp & Canoe in Maritime
Canada.* London: George Routledge & Sons Ltd., 1907.

CHAPTER 7   Samuels, Edward A. *With Fly-Rod & Camera.* New York:
Forest & Stream Publishing Co., 1890.

CHAPTER 8   Samuels. *With Fly-Rod & Camera.* 1890.

CHAPTER 9   *Morning Chronicle/Evening Echo*, "Road Map & Travelogue of
Nova Scotia." Halifax, N.S., 1924.
Paine, Albert Bigelow. *The Tent Dwellers.* 1908. Halifax: Nimbus
Publishing Limited, 1993.

ADDITIONAL SOURCES:
Chearnley, William. Unpublished papers, MG1, vol. 1464, #47.
Courtesy Ruth Holmes Whitehead, Nova Scotia Museum
of Natural History, Halifax, N.S.
Duncan, Francis. *Our Garrisons in the West.* London: Chapman & Hall,
1864.
Vieth, Frederick Harris D. *Recollections of the Crimean Campaign and the
Expedition to Kinburn in 1855 including also Sporting and
Dramatic Incidents in Connection with Garrison Life in the Canadian
Lower Province.* Montréal: John Lovell & Son Ltd., 1907.

CREDITS

Thanks to Nimbus Publishing; Peter Hope of Kejimkujik National Park; Ruth Holmes Whitehead of the Nova Scotia Museum of Natural History; Francis Hart and Ralph Watts of the Margaree Salmon Museum; staff of the Public Archives of Nova Scotia; Archive Photographic Reproduction Service; Beaton Institute, University College of Cape Breton; Legislative Library of Nova Scotia; Nova Scotia Department of Natural Resources; Mrs. Warren Miller; Maggie Nickerson; Clinton Miller; Gary and Barb MacDonald; Gary Castle; Ralph Stopps; as always Helen, Matthew and Emily.

PHOTO CREDITS

Identification of subject matter, if not given within the text, will follow each photo credit. If no details are available, it will be noted with 'anon.' Negative numbers are provided where possible.

CHAPTER 1

(p.4) Nova Scotia Museum (N. S. Museum); N-10,524.

(p.6) "A Hunters' Camp on Liverpool Chain of Lakes, Nova Scotia." Public Archives of Nova Scotia (PANS); N-7438; anon.

(p.8) N. S. Museum; N-10,682.

(p.11) Edward A. Samuels; *With Fly-Rod & Camera;* anon.

(p.13) PANS; N-2524.

(p.14) Clinton Miller, Bear River, N. S.; (Charlie Miller, centre of canoe; others, anon.).

(p.16) N. S. Museum; William Dennis Collection; N-14,778.

(p.18) PANS; N-7440; anon.

(p.20) Milford House.

(p.22) Clinton Miller, Bear River, N. S.; (foreground, Little John McEwan, John McEwan; others, anon. Moosehead Lake, ca. 1890s).

(p.24) PANS; N-7439; anon.

CHAPTER 2

(p.27) Kejimkujik National Park; Paul Yates Collection; N-27.

(p.28) Kejimkujik National Park; Paul Yates Collection; N-31.

(p.31) Personal Collection; anon.

(p.32) Milford House.

(p.33) Kejimkujik National Park; Paul Yates Collection; N-63; (Hardwood Carry); anon.

(p.35) Kejimkujik National Park; Paul Yates Collection; N-4; (Seth Mailman; Red Lake).

(p.37) Milford House.

(p.38) N. S. Museum; Genevieve Gloade Lowe Collection; N-11,256.

(p.39) Milford House.

(p.40) Kejimkujik National Park; Paul Yates Collection; N-3.

(p.41) Kejimkujik National Park; Paul Yates Collection; N-199.

(p.42) Milford House; anon.

CHAPTER 3

(p.47) Personal Collection; donated by Edith Gorst.

(p.48) Milford House.

(p.49) Kejimkujik National Park; Paul Yates Collection; N-156; (Irving Dam); anon.

(p.51) Colonel Sullivan, Southville, N. S. photo caption: In the Wilderness 1905–
the Doctor, Ned & Basil.

(p.52) PANS; St. Margarets Bay Historical Society Collection; ca. 1920; N-1864;
anon.

(p.54) Milford House.

CHAPTER 4

(p.57) PANS.

(p.58) PANS; W. C. Dunlop Collection.

(p.60) PANS; N-6824.

(p.62) Milford House; anon.

(p.64) N. S. Museum; N-10,683.

(p.66) PANS; N-6807; (L-R: 2 anon. sports; Micmac guides John Labrador,
Louis Peters, John McEwan).

(p.68) Personal Collection; (five Bear River Micmac guides; Johnnie McEwan,
centre; others anon.; camp location, unknown).

(p.69) Personal Collection; anon.

(p.71) Daniel Trueman Lecky, Berwick, N. S.

(p.72) PANS; N-6794.

(p.76) PANS; N-6809; (L-R: Bear River Micmac guides Louis Peters, John
McEwan, John McEwan, John Labrador; Bishop Jacqer's Camp, White Sand
Stream, Digby County; ca. 1890s).

(p.77) PANS; W. C. Dunlop Collection.

(p.78) PANS; Arthur Bloomfield Dawson Collection; N-139; Liscomb Mills; ca.
1921; anon.

(p.80) Bennie Morrison, Southville, N. S.

(p.81) PANS.

(p.85) PANS; N-3833; (Johnnie McEwan, second from right; others anon.).

(p.86) PANS; Arthur Bloomfield Dawson Collection; N-141; anon.

(p.88) Personal Collection; Ralph Harris photo; courtesy Grace Harris, Bear
River; (Micmac guide Billy Muise with unidentified sport).

CHAPTER 5

(p.90) Personal Collection; anon.

(p.92) PANS; W. C. Dunlop Collection; (Francis ?, Mrs. Martin Rosenburg; Sue's Place, near Chezzetcook, Halifax County; ca. 1899).

(p.94) PANS; W. C. Dunlop Collection; anon.; ca. 1899.

(p.96) Kejimkujik National Park; Paul Yates Collection; N-61; (Peskowesk); anon.

(p.97) PANS; W. C. Dunlop Collection; (Robert Finn, Anna Louise Russell; Officer's Lake, Halifax County; ca. 1899).

(p.98) Milford House; anon.

(p.100) N. S. Museum; N-11,008; (Indian camp at Bedford, N. S. ca. 1915); anon.

(p.102) Beaton Institute; College of Cape Breton.

(p.104) G. N. Tricoche; *Rambles Through the Maritime Provinces of Canada*.

(p.106) PANS; W. C. Dunlop Collection.

(p.108) Margaree Salmon Museum.

(p.110) Kejimkujik National Park; Paul Yates Collection; N-172; (Sixth Lake); anon.

(p.112) Kejimkujik National Park; Paul Yates Collection; N-8; (Red Lake); anon.

(p.115) PANS; W. C. Dunlop Collection; anon.; ca. 1900 (both photos).

(p.118) Kejimkujik National Park; Paul Yates Collection; N-41; (supper—three guides, Beaver Camp); anon.

CHAPTER 6

(p.122) PANS; N-6840; anon.

(p.124) Arthur P. Silver; *Farm-Cottage, Camp & Canoe in Maritime Canada*.

(p.126) Milford House.

(p.128) Milford House; anon.

CHAPTER 7

(p.131) Samuels; *With Fly-Rod & Camera;* anon.

(p.132) Maritime Museum of the Atlantic; N-17,539; Ralph Harris photo; (Bear River Micmac guide Billy Muise, stern of canoe, with unidentified sport).

CHAPTER 8

(p.135) Milford House; anon.

(p.136) Samuels; *With Fly-Rod & Camera;* anon.

(p.137) Samuels; *With Fly-Rod & Camera;* anon.

(p.138) Margaree Salmon Museum.

(p.140) Jim Alex Bennett, North East Margaree.

(p.142) Samuels; *With Fly-Rod & Camera;* anon.

(p.144) R. H. Brown fishing party at Indian Brook, Cape Breton, ca. 1897; Beaton Institute, University College of Cape Breton; anon.

(p.145) Margaree Salmon Museum; anon.

(p.146) Margaree Salmon Museum.

(p.149) Samuels; *With Fly-Rod & Camera.*

(p.150) PANS; W. C. Dunlop Collection; (Anna Louise Russell fishing at either Wild Cat Lake or Officers' Camp Lake near Chezzetcook, Halifax County; ca. 1899)

(151) Milford House; anon.

CHAPTER 9

(p.152) Milford House.

(p.153) Clinton Miller, Bear River, N. S.; (Fred Purdy's team at Lake Jolly, Digby County; ca. 1890s; anon.).

(p.154) Personal collection; (postcard from Ralph Harris photo).

(p.156) Milford House.

(p.157) Kejimkujik National Park; Paul Yates Collection; N-37; (Gorden Carry); anon.

(p.158) Milford House; anon.

(p.159) Milford House; anon.

(p.160) Kejimkujik National Park; Paul Yates Collection; N-146; anon.

(p.163) Kejimkujik National Park; Paul Yates Collection; N-113.

(p.164) Milford House.

(p.164) Milford House.

(p.165) Milford House.

(p.166) Milford House; (guides Charlie Sullivan and Lawrence Munro).

(p.167) Kejimkujik National Park; Paul Yates Collection; N-70; (Beaverskin Lake); anon.

(p.168) Milford House.

(p.169) Personal Collection; (postcard from Ralph Harris photo).

(p.171) Kejimkujik National Park; Paul Yates Collection; N-141.

(p.172) Milford House.

(p.173) Kejimkujik National Park; Paul Yates Collection; N-71; (Beaverskin Lake); anon.

(p.174) Kejimkujik National Park; Paul Yates Collection; N-155; (Irving Dam); anon.

(p.176) Kejimkujik National Park; Paul Yates Collection; N-177; (Wildcat Brook, guide Tom Canning with sport Howe).

(p.179) Kejimkujik National Park; Paul Yates Collection; N-82; (Sixth Lake, Digby County); anon.

(p.180) Maritime Museum of the Atlantic; Ralph Harris photo; N-17,539.